GARDENS OF SCOTLAND 1998

GW00492781

Conter

FRONT COVER PHOTOGRAPH

In the wild the giant Himalayan lily, *Cardiocrinum giganteum*, is found from Kashmir to north west Burma. The 5–11 foot high flower spikes carrying up to 25 fragrant, large white flowers grow in the mountains with Rhododendrons, Camellias, Magnolias and Bamboos. It was first discovered by Dr Wallich in 1816 and was introduced into cultivation around 1847. Unlike the true lilies the plant dies after flowering. Photographed in the walled garden at Logan Botanic Garden, Wigtownshire by Sidney J. Clarke, FRPS, Principal Photographer at the Royal Botanic Garden Edinburgh.

Illustrations by Steven Carroll

PRINTED BY INGLIS ALLEN, 40 TOWNSEND PLACE, KIRKCALDY, FIFE

2

CHAIRMAN'S MESSAGE

It was with tremendous pleasure that I was able to announce, at the end of a very happy and stimulating first year as Chairman of the Scheme, that we had clocked up another record total, and to give heartfelt congratulations and thanks to all our Organisers and Owners for this wonderful achievement.

I hope you will read the messages from our beneficiaries on the following pages which give an idea of what is done with the money which we pass on to them; as you can see, it is all put to very good use. Over and above this, there is, of course, the 40% which goes to our Owners' pet charities.

Our photographic competition, sponsored by Phillips, the Auctioneers, brought in some marvellous entries. As one of the judges, I know at first hand how difficult it was to choose between them, but I am sure you will agree that the winning photograph in the centre of the book is quite stunning.

The fact that you have bought our Yellow Book means that you enjoy visiting gardens, so please take along your friends and help us to make 1998 another bumper year.

❖❖

SCOTLAND'S GARDENS SCHEME HISTORY

Scotland's Gardens Scheme was founded on 23rd March 1931 at a garden owners' meeting called to help raise £2,000 which the Queen's Nursing Institute needed to fund the rapid expansion of district nursing. The Queen Mother, then the Duchess of York, lent her support, while King George V promised that the Balmoral gardens would open for the Scheme, with a generous annual contribution still being made today.

Under the inaugural chairmanship of the Countess of Minto, a central committee with a network of volunteer organisers throughout Scotland was formed, much the shape of the Scheme today. £1,000 was raised in the first year, double that in the next, and by 1939 over £22,000 was contributed. Even during the war proceeds increased, helped by the addition of flower and produce stalls and the provision of teas.

Although the training duties of the Queen's Nursing Institute were taken over by the National Health Service, many elderly nurses still receive our support. In 1952 the Gardens Fund of the National Trust for Scotland became our other main beneficiary, so that we could help to preserve the great gardens of historical importance in Scotland. In 1961 it was agreed that garden owners might select a registered charity to which up to 40% of the gross takings from their garden opening could be donated. This benefits over 150 different charities each year and is unique to Scotland's Gardens Scheme.

Over the years the Scheme has enabled millions of people to enjoy the beautiful gardens of Scotland and we hope, with your help, many more will do so for years to come.

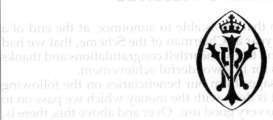

A MESSAGE FROM
THE QUEEN'S NURSING INSTITUTE, SCOTLAND

This year, thanks to the generous donation from Scotland's Gardens Scheme, we have again been able to increase our expenditure supporting the work of nurses in the community, currently having sixteen separate sponsorships operating throughout Scotland, from Shetland to the Borders.

The two year support towards outreach at **Rachel House**, the new Children's Hospice at Kinross, is nearly complete as is the support being given to community nurses involved with **Dementia** cases in the Inverness area. Collaboration with the **Multiple Sclerosis Society** of Scotland will enable a specialist nurse to work with newly diagnosed patients and their families in South Glasgow. To encourage individual nurses, **three Innovation Awards** have been given. The first is to provide health advice to those with learning disabilities at a Day Centre in Aberdeen, the second to assist bewildered, post consultative patients at a Health Centre in Dalkeith and the third for a nurse to work part of her time with MS patients in Morayshire.

We are particularly pleased with the system now in operation to monitor all these projects, from conception to conclusion, to ensure that the funding made available is used to maximum advantage.

We continue to assist with the training of community nurses and with research, as well as supporting retired Queen's Nurses all over Scotland. A leaflet outlining all the work of the Institute is available from Castle Terrace or from our new Website www.web13.co.uk/qnis, for the adventurous.

Our thanks to all those who toil to make this possible. We are told that stress causes more illness than anything else – there is nothing like a quiet spell, leaning on a hoe admiring nature's work, to relieve this.

George Preston   The Queen's Nursing Institute
Secretary & Treasurer   31 Castle Terrace, Edinburgh EH1 2EL

♔ The National Trust for Scotland

I am most grateful for this opportunity from Scotland's Gardens Scheme to extend a message to all associated with the Scheme. Although I was appointed Director in April 1997, I have been with the Trust for nearly sixteen years and in that time have appreciated very much the links between our two organisations. In particular, six years as Regional Director in Central and Tayside brought me into contact with many garden owners. This gave me a first hand appreciation of all the very hard work you put in and the vision and dedication with which you manage your gardens.

I often tell people in the Trust that you can lock up a building, or leave an area of open country for a month or so and the chances are that you will find it much as you left it – not so with a garden. A few weeks of neglect can take months to recover. Not everyone appreciates the arduous toil you put into your gardens and the fact that they are open to the public at certain times, from which the Trust and other charities benefit, is all the more to everyone's credit.

I am looking forward very much to working with the Gardens Scheme over the coming years. The close links between our two organisations are valued deeply. On behalf of The National Trust for Scotland, I would like to extend our sincere gratitude for the support which is given by Scotland's Gardens Scheme. Your help is of enormous significance to the Trust and is very much appreciated.

Trevor A Croft
Director

The Gardeners' Royal Benevolent Society in Scotland

An Exempt Charity Registered under the Industrial & Provident Societies Act 1965. Number 15408R.

The GRBS is a charitable organisation which has been helping retired gardeners and their partners for nearly 160 years. Today they give assistance to nearly 600 beneficiaries in the form of sheltered accommodation, quarterly payments, equipment, advice and holidays. Anyone who has earned his or her living in horticulture or gardening is eligible to apply for help.

In Scotland the Society offers sheltered housing at Netherbyres near Eyemouth in Berwickshire and a variety of accommodation in England from residential/nursing care to independent self-contained homes in West Sussex, Gloucestershire and Cambridgeshire.

Funds are always needed to continue our work. You can help by giving a donation, remembering the Society in your will or by shopping from the GRBS Gift catalogue. When you visit a garden in the *Gardens of Scotland* handbook, you are also contributing to the Society's funds. There are now four Regional Organisers in Scotland – please look out for them at gardening events during the year, they would be very glad to meet you.

Further information from Miss May Wardlaw, Development Officer for Scotland,
c/o SGS, 31 Castle Terrace, Edinburgh EH1 2EL *or*
The Gardeners' Royal Benevolent Society, Bridge House, 139 Kingston Road, Leatherhead, Surrey KT22 7NT.   Tel: 01372 373962 Fax: 01372 362575.

THE ROYAL GARDENERS' ORPHAN FUND
Registered Charity No. 248746

Established in 1887, in order to commemorate the Jubilee of Queen Victoria, the RGOF has been offering financial aid over the past 110 years to the orphaned children of professional horticulturists. In recent years the scope of our Fund has been widened so that assistance can now be offered to all needy children whose parents are or have been employed in horticulture.

During the past year we have helped seven orphaned children in Scotland. Our assistance to two of these children ended when they left school and college last summer to take up full time employment. We had been helping one of these children since his father died when he was five years old. Such a long term commitment could not be undertaken without the security of regular donations and we would like to take this opportunity of thanking all those who open their gardens for Scotland's Gardens Scheme for their hard work which makes the annual donation we receive from the Scheme possible.

For further information on the work of our Fund or to advise of any children who may qualify for our help please contact our Secretary, Mrs Kate Wallis, at:

48 St Albans Road, Codicote, Herts SG4 8UT   Tel: 01438 820783

GENERAL INFORMATION

Houses are not open unless specifically stated; where the house or part of the house is shown, an additional charge is usually made.

Lavatories. Private gardens do not normally have outside lavatories. Regrettably, for security reasons, owners have been advised not to admit visitors into their houses.

Dogs. Unless otherwise stated, dogs are usually admitted, but only if kept on a lead. They are not admitted to houses.

Teas. When teas are available this is indicated in the text. An extra charge is usually made for refreshments.

Professional Photographers. No photographs taken in a garden may be used for sale or reproduction without the prior permission of the garden owner.

♿ Denotes gardens suitable for wheelchairs.

\# Denotes gardens opening for the first time or re-opening after several years.

The National Trust for Scotland. Members are requested to note that where a National Trust property has allocated an opening day to Scotland's Gardens Scheme which is one of its own normal opening days, members can gain entry on production of their Trust membership card, although donations to Scotland's Gardens Scheme will be most welcome.

Children. All children must be accompanied by an adult.

SCOTLAND'S GARDENS SCHEME
Charity No. SC011337

We welcome gardens large and small and also groups of gardens.
If you would like information on how to open your garden for charity
please contact us at the address below.

SCOTLAND'S GARDENS SCHEME,
31 CASTLE TERRACE, EDINBURGH
Telephone: 0131 229 1870   Fax: 0131 229 0443

NAME & ADDRESS: (Block capitals please) ....

....

....

.... Postcode ....

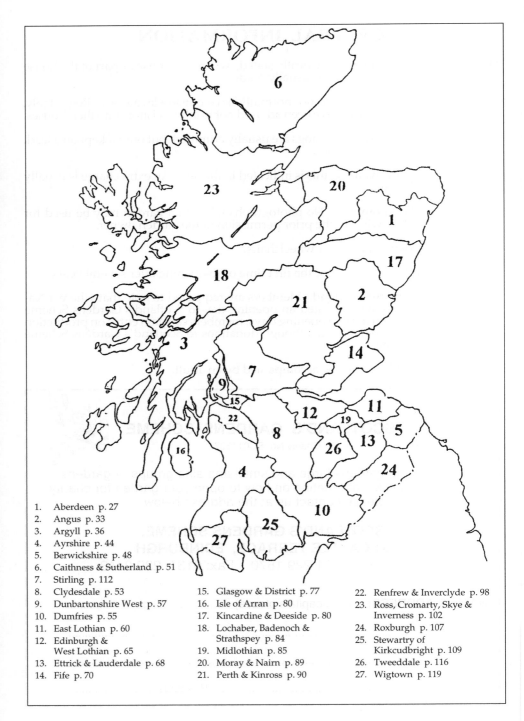

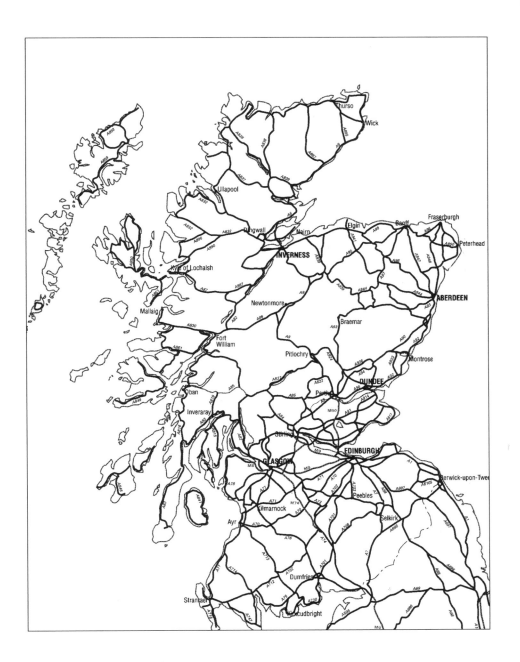

GARDENS OPEN ON A REGULAR BASIS or BY APPOINTMENT

Full details are given in the District List of Gardens

ABERDEEN

23 Don Street, Old Aberdeen   *Daily April–September by appointment: 01224 487269*
#Daluaine, Rhynie   *April–November by appointment: 01464 861638*
Greenridge, Cults   *July & August by appointment: 01224 860200*
Nether Affloch Farmhouse, Dunecht   *July & August by appointment: 01330 860362*
Station Cottage, Gartly   *July & August by appointment: 01466 720277*

ANGUS

House of Pitmuies, Guthrie,   *Daily 1 April – 31 October 10am-5pm*

ARGYLL

Achnacloich, Connel   *Daily 6 April – 31 October 10am - 6pm*
An Cala, Ellenabeich   *Daily 1 April-15 October 10am - 6pm*
Appin House, Appin   *Daily 13 April - 11 October 10am - 6pm*
Ardanaiseig, Lochaweside   *Daily all year 9am - 5pm*
Ardchattan Priory, North Connel   *Daily 1 April-30 October 9am - 6pm*
Ardkinglas Woodland Garden, Cairndow   *Daily all year*
Ardmaddy Castle, Balvicar   *Daily all year 9am–sunset, or by appt: 01852 300353*
#Ascog Hall, Isle of Bute   *Daily (except Mon & Tues) mid April – mid Octoebr 10am – 6pm*
Barguillean's 'Angus Garden', Taynuilt   *Daily all year*
Cnoc-na-Garrie, Ballymeanoch *First Wednesday April – October 2–6pm or by appt: 01546 605327*
Coille Dharaich, Kilmelford   *April – September by appointment: 01852 200285*
Crarae Glen Garden, Minard   *Daily April-October 9am - 6pm*
Crinan Hotel Garden, Crinan   *Daily 30 April - 30 September*
Dalnaheish, Tayvallich   *April–September by appointment: 01546   870286*
Druimavuic House, Appin   *Daily 5April–29 June 10am - 6 pm*
Druimneil House, Port Appin   *Daily Easter – October 9am - 6pm*
Eredine Woodland Garden, Lochaweside   *Saturdays all year, except 6 June, 11am - 4pm*
Jura House, Isle of Jura   *Open all year 9am - 5pm*
Kildalloig, Campbeltown   *By appointment: 01586 553192*
Kinlochlaich House Gardens, Appin   *Open all year 9.30am-5.30pm or dusk (except Suns Oct–March)*
                                         Sundays April - Sept. 10.30am - 5.30pm
Mount Stuart, Isle of Bute   *10–13 April & 1 May - 18 October (not Tues & Thurs) 10am-5pm.*
Tighnamara, Kilmelford   *By appointment spring - autumn: 01852 200224*
Torosay Castle & Gardens, Isle of Mull   *Open all year. Summer 9am - 7pm.Winter, sunrise - sunset*

AYRSHIRE

Bargany, Girvan   *1 March–31 October 10am-7pm or dusk*
Blair, Dalry   *All year round*

BERWICKSHIRE

Bughtrig, Leitholm   *June – September 11am-5pm or by appointment: 01890 840678*
The Hirsel, Coldstream   *Open daily all year reasonable daylight hours*
Manderston, Duns   *Sundays & Thursdays 14 May-27 September*
Netherbyres, Eyemouth   *Parties of 10 or more by appointment: 01890 750337*

CLYDESDALE

Baitlaws, Lamington *July & August by appointment: 01899 850240*
Biggar Park, Biggar *By appointment: 01899 220185*

DUMFRIES

Arbigland, Kirkbean *Tuesdays-Sundays: May-September 2-6pm Also Bank Holiday Mondays*

DUNBARTONSHIRE WEST

Auchendarroch, Tarbet *1 April – 31 August by appointment: 01301 702240*
Glenarn, Rhu *Daily 21 March-21 September, Sunrise to Sunset*

EDINBURGH & WEST LOTHIAN

13 Belford Place, *Edinburgh 1st April – 31st July by appointment: 0131 332 2104*
Newliston, Kirkliston *Wednesdays-Sundays incl. 1May- 4 June 2-6pm*

FIFE

Cambo House, Kingsbarns *Daily all year 10am-5pm*

GLASGOW

Bystone Mews, Clarkston *May – August by appointment: 0141 644 1856*
Invermay, Cambuslang *April – September by appointment: 0141 641 1632*
Six Fathoms, Eaglesham *July & August by appointment: 01355 302321*

KINCARDINE & DEESIDE

Shooting Greens, Strachan *27 April – 10 May by appointment: 01330 850221*

MIDLOTHIAN

Greenfield Lodge, Lasswade *First Tuesday of each month March-September incl. 2-5pm,*
                                or by appointment: 0131 663 9338
The Mill House, Temple *Second Wednesday of each month April-September incl. 2-5pm*
Newhall, Carlops *Tuesdays to Thursdays, April - October. Glen 1-5pm Walled Garden 2-5pm*

PERTH AND KINROSS

Ardvorlich, Lochearnhead *10 May – 7 June 2 - 6pm*
Bolfracks, Aberfeldy *Daily 1 April – 31 October 10am - 6pm*
Cluny House, Aberfeldy *Daily 1 March – 31 October 10am - 6pm*
Drummond Castle Gardens, Muthill *Daily May–October 2 - 6pm,last entrance 5pm*
Scone Palace, Perth *10 April – 12 October 9.30am – 5.15pm, last entrance 4.45pm*
Wester Dalqueich, Carnbo *By appointment, parties of 10 or more, late May–August: 01577 840229*

RENFREW & INVERCLYDE

31 Kings Road, Elderslie *By appointment April – June: 01505 320480*
Crossways, Bishopton *First Sunday March – September*

ROSS, CROMARTY, SKYE & INVERNESS

Abriachan Garden Nursery, Loch Ness side   *February-November 9am - dusk*
Attadale, Strathcarron   *Easter - end October, not Suns 10am-5pm*
Clan Donald, Isle of Skye   *Daily all year*
Coiltie, Divach, Drumnadrochit   *Daily 16 May – 31 July 12-7pm*
Dunvegan Castle, Isle of Skye   *23 March-31 October 10am-5pm, Nov – March 11am–3.30pm*
Glamaig, Isle of Skye   *Daily Easter to mid September*
Leckmelm Shrubbery & Arboretum by Ullapool   *Daily 1 April-30 September 10am - 6pm*
Sea View, Dundonnell   *May to September, or by appointment:01854 633317*
Tournaig, Poolewe   *By appointment: 01445 781250 or 781339*

ROXBURGH

Floors Castle, Kelso   *Daily Easter – end October 10am – 4.30pm*

STEWARTRY OF KIRKCUDBRIGHT

Barnhourie Mill, Colvend   *By appointment: 01387 780269*
Corsock House, Castle Douglas   *By appointment: 01644 440250*

STIRLING

Daldrishaig House, Aberfoyle   *May to July by appointment: 01877 382223*
Kilbryde Castle, Dunblane   *All year by appointment: 01786 823104*

TWEEDDALE

Glenhighton, Broughton   *Last Thursday June – September 12.30 – 5pm*
Kailzie Gardens, Peebles   *Daily 21March – 17 October 11am-5.30pm*
Winter: Daylight hours, gardens only

WIGTOWN

Ardwell House Gardens, Ardwell   *Daily 1April – 30 September 10am-5pm*
Castle Kennedy & Lochinch Gardens   *Daily 1 April – 30 September 10am-5pm*
Whitehills Garden & Nursery, Newton Stewart   *Daily 1 April - 31 October by appt: 01671 402049*

MONTHLY CALENDAR LIST

FEBRUARY

MARCH

APRIL

MAY

SATURDAY 2nd MAY

SUNDAY 3rd MAY

TUESDAY 5th MAY

WEDNESDAY 6th MAY

SATURDAY 9th MAY

SATURDAY & SUNDAY 9th & 10th MAY

SUNDAY 10th MAY

WEDNESDAY 13th MAY

THURSDAY 14th MAY

SATURDAY & SUNDAY 30th & 31st MAY

SUNDAY 31st MAY

JUNE

TUESDAY 2nd JUNE

WEDNESDAY 3rd JUNE

SATURDAY 6th JUNE

SATURDAY & SUNDAY 6th & 7th JUNE

SUNDAY 7th JUNE

WEDNESDAY 10th JUNE

FRIDAY & SATURDAY 12th & 13th JUNE

SATURDAY 13th JUNE

SATURDAY & SUNDAY 13th & 14th JUNE

SUNDAY 14th JUNE

SATURDAY 20th JUNE

SUNDAY 21st JUNE

WEDNESDAY 24th JUNE

THURSDAY 25th JUNE

SATURDAY 27th JUNE

SATURDAY & SUNDAY 27th & 28th JUNE

SUNDAY 28th JUNE

SATURDAY & SUNDAY 18th & 19th JULY

SUNDAY 19th JULY

WEDNESDAY 22nd JULY

SATURDAY & SUNDAY 25th & 26th JULY

SUNDAY 26th JULY

THURSDAY 30th JULY

AUGUST

SATURDAY 1st AUGUST

SATURDAY & SUNDAY 1st & 2nd AUGUST

SUNDAY 2nd AUGUST

TUESDAY 4th AUGUST

WEDNESDAY 5th AUGUST

SATURDAY & SUNDAY 8th & 9th AUGUST

SATURDAY 8th – SUNDAY 16th AUGUST

SUNDAY 9th AUGUST

WEDNESDAY 12th AUGUST

SATURDAY 15th AUGUST

SATURDAY & SUNDAY 15th & 16th AUGUST

SUNDAY 16th AUGUST

PLANT SALES in 1998

Bring & Buy!
Bargain Prices!   Free Expert Advice!

Renfrew & Inverclyde: **CARRUTH, Bridge of Weir**
Sunday 31 MAY 2 – 5pm

Fife: **KARBET, Freuchie**
Sunday 7 JUNE 11am – 4pm

Dunbartonshire West: **THE HILL HOUSE, Helensburgh**
Sunday 6 SEPTEMBER 11am – 5pm

Edinburgh & West Lothian: **KIRKNEWTON HOUSE**
Saturday & Sunday 26 & 27 SEPTEMBER
11.30am – 4pm

Fife: **HILL OF TARVIT, Cupar**
Saturday 3 OCTOBER 10.30am – 4pm
Sunday 4 OCTOBER 1 – 4pm

Midlothian: **OXENFOORD MAINS, Dalkeith**
Saturday 10 OCTOBER 1 – 4pm
Sunday 11 OCTOBER 10.30am – 3pm

ABERDEEN

District Organiser *& Hon. Treasurer:*	**Mrs David James Duff,** Hatton Castle, Turriff AB53 8ED
Area Organisers:	**Mrs W Bruce,** Logie House, Ellon AB41 8LH **Mrs D M Crichton Maitland**, Daluaine, Rhynie AB54 4HL **Mrs F G Lawson,** Asloun, Alford AB33 8NR **Mrs A Robertson,** Drumblade House, Huntly AB54 6ER **Mrs F M K Tuck**, Allargue House, Corgarff AB36 8YP

DATES OF OPENING

23 Don Street, Old Aberdeen .... April – September by appt.
Daluaine, Rhynie .... April – November by appt.
Greenridge, Cults .... July & August by appt.
Nether Affloch Farmhouse, Dunecht .... July & August by appt.
Station Cottage, Gartly .... June - August by appt.

Auchmacoy, Ellon	Sunday 19 April	1.30 – 4.30pm
Culquoich, Alford	Sunday 24 May	1.30 – 5pm
Grandhome, Aberdeen	Sunday 24 May	2 – 5pm
Dunlugas, Turriff	Sunday 31 May	2 – 6pm
Scatterty, Turriff	Sunday 31 May	2 – 6pm
Kildrummy Castle Gardens, Alford	Sunday 7 June	10am – 5pm
Dunecht House Garden, Dunecht	Sunday 7 June	1 – 5pm
Dunecht House Garden, Dunecht	Sunday 14 June	1 – 5pm
Howemill, Craigievar, Alford	Sunday 21 June	1.30 – 5pm
Ploughman's Hall, Old Rayne	Sunday 5 July	1 – 6pm
Waterside Farmhouse, Oyne	Sunday 5 July	1 – 6pm
23 Don Street, Old Aberdeen	Sunday 12 July	1.30 – 6pm
Leith Hall, Kennethmont, by Huntly	Sunday 19 July	1.30 – 5pm
Candacraig, Strathdon	Sunday 26 July	2 – 6pm
Castle Fraser, Kemnay	Sunday 26 July	2 – 5pm
Esslemont, Ellon	Sunday 2 August	1 – 5pm
Old Leslie, by Insch	Sunday 2 August	1 – 5pm
Haddo House, Tarves	Sunday 9 August	2 – 5pm
Pitmedden Gardens, Pitmedden	Sunday 16 August	10 – 5.30pm
Dunecht House Garden, Dunecht	Sunday 23 August	1 – 5pm
Tillypronie, Tarland	Sunday 30 August	2 – 5pm

23 DON STREET, Old Aberdeen &

(Miss M Mackechnie)
A secret small walled garden in historic Old Aberdeen. Recently shown on 'The Beechgrove Garden'. Wide range of rare and unusual plants and old-fashioned roses. Small pool with aquatic plants. Park at St Machar Cathedral, short walk down Chanonry to Don Street, turn right. City plan ref: P7.
Admission £1.60 Concessions £1.10 Full afternoon tea £2.00.
OPEN APRIL TO SEPTEMBER BY APPOINTMENT Tel: 01224 487269.
SUNDAY 12th JULY 1.30 – 6pm
40% to Cat Protection League

AUCHMACOY, Ellon &

(Captain D W S Buchan)
Auchmacoy House policies feature an attractive display of tens of thousands of daffodils. Home made teas. Plant stall.
Admission £2.00 Children & OAPs 50p
SUNDAY 19th APRIL 1.30 – 4.30 pm
40% to Gordon Highlanders Museum Appeal

CANDACRAIG NURSERY GARDEN, Strathdon & (limited)

Walled garden with wild flower meadow, natural pond, formal herbaceous borders and terrace walk. Wide range of plants on view and for sale. Newly restored Victorian Gothic summerhouse now houses art gallery with varying exhibitions during summer months. Marquee teas. ¼ m west of Rough Park garage on A944.
Admission £1.50 Concessions £1.00 Children free
SUNDAY 26th JULY 2 - 6pm
40% to Concern World Wide

CASTLE FRASER, Kemnay &

(The National Trust for Scotland)
Castle Fraser, one of the most spectacular of the Castles of Mar, belongs to the same period of native architectural achievements as Crathes Castle and Craigievar Castle. The walled garden has been fully restored by the Trust and forms a delightful adjunct to the Castle. Plant & vegetable sales. Tea room. Woodland walks, adventure playground. Near Kemnay, off A944.
Admission £2.00 Children £1.30
SUNDAY 26th JULY 2 – 5 pm
40% to The Gardens Fund of The National Trust for Scotland
For other opening details see page 133

CULQUOICH, Alford

(Mrs M I Bell Tawse)
Natural woodlands, including an interesting pinetum, shrubs, spring bulbs, azaleas and rhododendrons. Tea and biscuits. Garden is west of Glenkindie village, opposite Glenkindie House, off main Alford-Strathdon road, A97.
Admission £1.00
SUNDAY 24th MAY 1.30 – 5 pm
40% to Arthritis and Rheumatism Council

 # DALUAINE, Rhynie &
(Major & Mrs Crichton Maitland)
Young garden. Formal 17th century walled garden, closely planted with interesting
herbaceous, roses and shrubs. Small woodland area with rare trees, specie
rhododendrons, bulbs and primulas. New 3-acre arboretum along the River Bogie.
Good collection of trees and conifers. Teas by arrangement. Bus parties welcome. No
dogs please. Off A97 in Rhynie. Manse Road, 9 miles south of Huntly, opposite Richard
Arms Hotel.
Admission £2.00 Children £1.00
By appointment 1st APRIL – 1st NOVEMBER Tel: 01464 861638
40% to R N L I

DUNECHT HOUSE GARDENS, Dunecht & (partly)
(The Hon Charles A Pearson)
Romanesque addition, 1877, by G Edmund Street, to original House by John & William
Smith. Herbaceous borders, heath and wild garden. Light refreshments. Cars free.
Dunecht 1 mile. Routes A974, A944, B 977.
Admission £2.00 Children £1.00
SUNDAY 7th and SUNDAY 14th JUNE 1 – 5 pm
40% to Queen's Nursing Institute (Scotland)
SUNDAY 23rd AUGUST 1 – 5 pm
40% to Aberdeen Branch Riding for the Disabled

DUNLUGAS, Turriff & (partly)
(Mr & Mrs J Stancioff)
Wild garden with woodland walks, water garden and walled garden. Turn off B9025 at
east side of Turriff bridge, 4 miles along on left. NB Scattery garden, ½ mile north, is also
open.
Admission £2.00 Teas £1.50.
SUNDAY 31st MAY 2 – 6pm
40% to Friends of Turriff Hospital

ESSLEMONT, Ellon &
(Mrs Robert Wolrige Gordon of Esslemont)
Victorian house set in wooded policies above River Ythan. Roses and shrubs in garden
with double yew hedges (17th and 18th centuries). Music, stalls, charity stalls. Home
baked teas. Ellon 2 miles. Take A920 from Ellon. On Pitmedden/Oldmeldrum road.
Admission: Cars £2.00
SUNDAY 2nd AUGUST 1 – 5 pm
15% to Hearing Dogs for the Deaf, 15% to Leonard Cheshire Foundation in Scotland,
10% between Tarves Boys' Brigade and St Mary on the Rock Graveyard.

GRANDHOME, Aberdeen &
(Mr & Mrs D R Paton)
18th century walled garden, incorporating rose garden; policies with rhododendrons,
azaleas, mature trees and shrubs. Plant stall. Teas. From Aberdeen via Persley Bridge,
turn left at Danestone Shopping Centre roundabout.
Admission £2.00 Children & OAPs £1.00
SUNDAY 24th MAY 2 – 5pm
40% to Children First

GREENRIDGE, Craigton Road, Cults
(BP Exploration Co Ltd)
Large secluded garden surrounding 1840 Archibald Simpson house, for many years winner of Britain in Bloom 'Best Hidden Garden'. Mature specimen trees and shrubs. Sloping walled rose garden and terraces. Kitchen garden. Teas. Plant stall.
Admission £3.50 including tea
JULY and AUGUST by appointment. Tel: 01224 860200 Fax: 01224 860210
40% to Association of the Friends of Raeden

HADDO HOUSE, Tarves ♿
(The National Trust for Scotland)
A delightful terraced garden of rosebeds and herbaceous borders leads into a magnificent Country Park with lakes, walks and monuments. Shops and restaurant. Off B999 4 miles north of Pitmedden, 19 miles north of Aberdeen.
Admission £1.50 Children free
SUNDAY 9th AUGUST 2 - 5pm
40% to The Gardens Fund of the National Trust for Scotland

HOWEMILL, Craigievar ♿ with help
(Mr D Atkinson)
Expanding garden with a wide range of unusual alpines, shrubs and herbaceous plants. Plant stall. Teas. From Alford take A980 Alford/Lumphanan road.
No dogs please.
Admission £1.50 Children under 12 free
SUNDAY 21st JUNE 1.30 - 5pm
40% to Cancer Relief Macmillan Fund

KILDRUMMY CASTLE GARDENS, Alford ♿ (with help)
(Kildrummy Garden Trust)
April shows the gold of the lysichitons in the water garden, and the small bulbs naturalised beside the copy of the 14th century Brig o' Balgownie. Rhododendrons and azaleas from April (frost permitting). September/October brings colchicums and brilliant colour with acers, fothergillas and viburnums. Plants for sale. Play area. Video room. Wheelchair facilities. Car park free inside hotel main entrance. Coach park up hotel delivery entrance. Parties by arrangement. Open daily April - October.
Tel: 01975 571277/571203. On A97, 10 miles from Alford, 17 miles from Huntly.
Admission £2.00 Children free
SUNDAY 7th JUNE 10 am – 5 pm
40% to Fabric Fund, Kildrummy Church.

LEITH HALL, Kennethmont
(The National Trust for Scotland)
This attractive old country house, the earliest part of which dates from 1650, was the home of the Leith and Leith-Hay families for more than three centuries. The west garden was made by Mr and The Hon. Mrs Charles Leith-Hay around the beginning of the twentieth century. The property was given to the Trust in 1945. The rock garden has been enhanced by the Scottish Rock Garden Club in celebration of their 150th anniversary. Toilet for disabled visitors. Teas. Pipe band. On B9002 near Kennethmont.
Admission £2.00 Children & OAPs £1.30
SUNDAY 19th JULY 1.30 – 5pm
40% to The Gardens Fund of The National Trust for Scotland
For details of other openings see page 130

NETHER AFFLOCH FARMHOUSE, Dunecht   ৬ (with help)
(Mr & Mrs M J Reid)
19th century renovated cottage garden with large collection of climbing roses. Fine
views, mature trees, herbaceous borders. Unusual plants, many varieties of old
fashioned and specie roses, herbs and alpines. Plants for sale. Groups very welcome.
Sorry no dogs. Route A944.
Admission £2.00
JULY & AUGUST, by appointment. Tel. 01330 860362
40% to Ménière's Society

 # OLD LESLIE HOUSE, by Insch   ৬ (with help)
(Mr & Mrs M Strachan)
Developing two-acre garden featuring mixed borders, rock garden and watercourse.
Small woodland garden with fine views of Bennachie. Teas. Plant stall. No dogs please.
Leave A96 at B9002, direction Kennethmont. First left after intersection with B992. In
Old Leslie turn left at T-junction, garden is 100 yards on the left.
Admission £2.00 Children £1.00
SUNDAY 2nd AUGUST 1 – 5pm
20% to R N L I   20% to Imperial Cancer Research

PITMEDDEN GARDEN, Ellon ৬
(The National Trust for Scotland)
Garden created by Lord Pitmedden in 1675. Elaborate floral designs in parterres of box
edging, inspired by the garden at the Palace of Holyroodhouse, have been re-created by
the Trust. Fountains and sundials make fine centrepieces to the garden, filled in summer
with 40,000 annual flowers. Also Museum of Farming Life, Visitor Centre, woodland
walk. Tearoom. Special rates for pre-booked coach parties.
Admission £3.70 Concessions & children £2.50 Family £9.90.
SUNDAY 16th AUGUST 10am – 5pm
40% to The Gardens Fund of The National Trust for Scotland
For details of other openings see page 131

PLOUGHMAN'S HALL, Old Rayne ৬ with help
(Mr & Mrs A Gardner)
One acre garden. Rock, herbaceous, kitchen, woodland and dried flower gardens. Plant
stall. Off A96, 9 miles north of Inverurie.
JOINT OPENING WITH WATERSIDE FARMHOUSE, OYNE
Admission £1.50 Children 50p
SUNDAY 5th JULY 1 - 6pm
40% to Wycliffe Bible Translators

 # SCATTERTY, Turriff
(Alexander Urquhart)
Informal garden, about 2 acres on different levels. Indigenous plants plus a number of
rare trees and shrubs; bamboos and sorbus. Pond and stream and a planted courtyard.
NB ½ north of Dunlugas garden opening same day.
Admission £2.00 Children 75p
SUNDAY 31st MAY 2 – 6pm
40% to Childrens Hospice Association Scotland

STATION COTTAGE, Gartly
(Travers & Betty Cosgrove)
Century old quarry converted into a "secret garden" by generations of railwaymen. Old cottage plants. Climbing pathways through wild garden. Railway site preserved. Plants for sale. Railway still in use. 5 miles south of Huntly on A97 towards Rhynie. Follow signs for Gartly from A96.
Admission £1.00 Children & OAPs 50p
JULY and AUGUST by appointment. Tel: 01466 720277
40% to Parish of Noth, Church of Scotland

TILLYPRONIE, Tarland ♿
(The Hon Philip Astor)
Late Victorian house. Herbaceous borders, terraced garden with pond at bottom. Shrubs, heaths and ornamental trees in pinetum. Vegetable garden. Superb views. Picnic area. Free car park. Dogs on lead, please. Teas.
Admission £1.50 Children 75p
SUNDAY 30th AUGUST 2 – 5 pm
All proceeds to Scotland's Gardens Scheme

WATERSIDE FARMHOUSE, Oyne
(Ann & Colin Millar)
A developing garden, started in 1991 from a rough farmyard. Recently planted woodland extends to 2 acres around 19th century farmhouse and courtyard with cordoned fruit trees and kitchen garden. Mixed shrub and herbaceous borders, pond, heathers and herbs. Teas. No dogs please. Off A96, ½ mile north of junction with B9002.
JOINT OPENING WITH PLOUGHMAN'S HALL, OLD RAYNE
Admission £1.50 Children 50p
SUNDAY 5th JULY 1 - 6pm
40% to Books Abroad

We welcome new gardens of all shapes and sizes,
opening in a group or alone,
for one day or for many ....
Complete the form on page 7 and return to us
and we will send you our information pack.

ANGUS

District Organiser:	**Mrs Jonathan Stansfeld**, Dunninald, by Montrose DD10 9TD
Area Organisers:	**Miss Ruth Dundas,** Caddam, Kinnordy, Kirriemuir DD8 4LP
	Mrs R J Ephraums, Damside, Leysmill, Arbroath DD11 4RS
	Mrs A Houstoun, Kerbet House, Kinnettles, Forfar DD8 1TQ
	Mrs R H B Learoyd, Priestoun, Edzell DD9 7UD
	Mrs T D Lloyd-Jones, Reswallie House, by Forfar DD8 2SA
Hon. Treasurer:	**Col R H B Learoyd,** Priestoun, Edzell DD9 7UD

DATES OF OPENING

House of Pitmuies, Guthrie, by Forfar .... 1 April to 31 October   10am–5pm

Brechin Castle, Brechin	Sunday 24 May	2–5.30pm
Drumkilbo, Meigle	Sunday 31 May	2–5.30pm
Cortachy Castle, Kirriemuir	Sunday 7 June	2 – 6pm
Kinnettles House, by Forfar	Sunday 7 June	2 – 6pm
Reswallie, by Forfar	Sunday 21 June	2–5.30pm
House of Dun, Montrose	Saturday 27 June	12.30–5pm
Newtonmill, by Edzell	Sunday 28 June	2–5.30pm
Newtyle Village	Sunday 28 June	1–5.30pm
Brechin Castle, Brechin	Sunday 5 July	2–5.30pm
Glamis Castle	Sunday 5 July	10am–5.30pm
Edzell Village & Edzell Castle	Sunday 26 July	1.30–5.30pm
Kinpurnie Castle, Newtyle	Sunday 2 August	2 – 6pm

BRECHIN CASTLE, Brechin
(The Earl of Dalhousie)
Ancient fortress of Scottish kings on cliff overlooking River Southesk. Rebuilt by
Alexander Edward - completed in 1711. Extensive walled garden half a mile from Castle
with ancient and new plantings and mown lawn approach. Rhododendrons, azaleas,
bulbs, interesting trees, wild garden. Tea in garden. Car parking free.
Route A90.
Admission £2 Children over 5 50p
SUNDAY 24th MAY and SUNDAY 5th July 2 - 5.30pm
15% to RSSPC, 15% to Save the Children Fund, 10% to NCCPG

CORTACHY CASTLE, Kirriemuir
 (The Earl & Countess of Airlie)
16th century castellated house. Additions in 1872 by David Bryce. Spring garden and
wild pond garden with azaleas, primroses and rhododendrons. Garden of fine American
specie trees and river walk along South Esk. Teas. Garden quiz.
Kirriemuir 5 miles. Route B955.
Admission £1.75 Children 25p
SUNDAY 7th JUNE 2 - 6 pm
40% between The Leonard Cheshire Foundation (Scotland) and RNLI Arbroath

DRUMKILBO, Meigle ♿

(Mr G & Mrs V Bunting)

Older trees date to pre-war years of John Cox, as do the structures of the front garden designed by Sir Robert Lorimer in 1920. The formal garden with specimen azaleas and rhododendrons was created by the 17th Lord Elphinstone between 1951 and 1970. Teas. Plant stall. Route A94, Meigle 1 mile. Bus: Dundee/Blairgowrie, via Alyth.
Admission £1.75 Children 25p
SUNDAY 31st MAY 2 – 5.30pm
40% to King George's Fund for Sailors

EDZELL VILLAGE & EDZELL CASTLE

Walk round 10 gardens in Edzell village. Edzell Castle is also on view. Teas extra. Tickets are on sale in the village and a plan is issued with the tickets. Piper. Plant stall.
Admission £2.00 Children 50p
SUNDAY 26th JULY 1.30 - 5.30 pm
20% to Chest, Heart & Stroke Association   20% to Belarus Appeal

---

GLAMIS CASTLE, Glamis ♿

(The Earl & Countess of Strathmore & Kinghorne)

Family home of the Earls of Strathmore and a royal residence since 1372. Childhood home of HM Queen Elizabeth The Queen Mother, birthplace of HRH The Princess Margaret, and legendary setting for Shakespeare's play 'Macbeth'. Five-storey L-shaped tower block dating from 15th century, remodelled 1600, containing magnificent rooms with wide range of historic pictures, furniture, porcelain etc. Spacious grounds with river and woodland paths. Nature trail. Impressive policy timbers. Formal garden. Restaurant. Teas. Four gift shops. Glamis 1 mile A94.
Admission to Castle & grounds: £5.20, OAPs £4.00, children £2.70.

Admission: Grounds only £2.40
Children & OAPs £1.30
SUNDAY 5th JULY 10am - 5.30pm
40% to The Leonard Cheshire Foundation in Scotland

HOUSE OF DUN, Montrose ♿

(The National Trust for Scotland)

William Adam not only designed this beautiful country house, but also the landscape surrounding it. The restored walled garden displays lovely period herbaceous and rose borders while the avenues and the ha-ha are the original surviving features. *Wellingtonias* present a striking entrance to the north of the house and the Den offers a pleasant and restful woodland walk. Plant stall. Tearoom. Off A935 3 miles west of Montrose. Admission to House & Garden: £3.70 Concessions £2.50 Family Group £9.90.
Garden & grounds only £1.00
SATURDAY 27th JUNE 12.30pm - 5pm
40% to The Gardens Fund of The National Trust for Scotland

HOUSE OF PITMUIES, Guthrie, by Forfar
(Mrs Farquhar Ogilvie)
Semi-formal old walled gardens adjoining 18th century house. Massed spring bulbs, roses, herbaceous borders and a wide variety of shrubs. Old fashioned roses in summer with long borders of herbaceous perennials and superb delphiniums. Riverside walk with fine trees, interesting turreted doocot and "Gothic" wash-house. Dogs on lead please. Rare & unusual plants for sale. Fruit in season. Friockheim 1½m Route A932. Admission £2.00
1 APRIL to 31st OCTOBER 10 am - 5 pm
Donation to Scotland's Gardens Scheme

KINNETTLES HOUSE, Douglastown, by Forfar
(Mr & Mrs Hugh Walker-Munro)
Rhododendron walk and rare trees and a mausoleum where an Indian princess is said to be buried. Formal terraced garden. Three miles south of Forfar on A94. Signed from main road or Dundee/Forfar road, 8 miles. Follow signs for Douglastown. Admission £1.50 Children free
SUNDAY 7th JUNE 2 - 6pm
40% to Kinnettles Village Hall

KINPURNIE CASTLE, Newtyle
(Sir James Cayzer Bt)
Early 20th century house (not open). Panoramic views of the vale of Strathmore and the Grampians. Shrubs and herbaceous garden. The Ladies Palm Court Orchestra will play. Route B954. Dundee 10 m. Perth 18 m.
Admission £1.50 Children 50p
SUNDAY 2nd AUGUST 2 - 6 pm
40% to Angus branch, British Red Cross

NEWTONMILL HOUSE, by Edzell   ♿
(Mr & Mrs Stephen Rickman)
A walled garden comprising herbaceous borders, rose and peony beds, vegetable beds and doocot. Formal layout with view to house. Plant stall. Teas. No dogs please. B966 Brechin/Edzell road.
Admission £1.75 Children 50p
SUNDAY 28th JUNE 2 – 5.30pm
40% to Scottish Dyslexia Association

NEWTYLE VILLAGE   ♿ (with assistance)
Several cottage gardens, planted in a variety of styles, may be visited in the course of a short walk round the village of Newtyle. The village, with its regular street plan, was laid out in 1832 next to the northern terminus of Scotland's first passenger railway. Tickets on sale at the Church Hall. Plants for sale. Teas in Church Hall. Newtyle is on B954 between Meigle and Dundee, 2 miles off A94 between Coupar Angus and Glamis. Admission includes all gardens: £2.00 Children under 12 free
Teas: Adults & children £1.00
SUNDAY 28th JUNE 1 – 5.30pm
20% to Alzheimer's Scotland (Angus branch)   *20% to Newtyle Church of Scotland*

RESWALLIE, by Forfar ♿
(Col & Mrs T D Lloyd-Jones)
18th century house set in policies of 120 acres. Woodland walks with many interesting trees. Walled herbaceous garden. Vintage cars and motor cycles on display. Plant stall. Teas. Free car parking. Off A932 Forfar/Friockheim. Reswallie signposted to left.
Admission £1.50 Children 50p
SUNDAY 21st JUNE 2 – 5.30pm
40% to British Red Cross Society (Angus branch)

ARGYLL

District Organiser *& Hon Treasurer:*	**Mrs C Struthers,** Ardmaddy Castle, Balvicar PA34 4QY
Area Organisers:	**Mrs Charles Gore**, Port na Mine, Taynuilt PA35 1HU **Mrs E B Ingleby,** Braighbhaille, Crarae, Inveraray PA32 8YA **Mrs A Staunton,** Ardare, Colintraive PA22 3AS

DATES OF OPENING

Achnacloich, Connel	Daily 6 April–31 October	10am – 6pm
An Cala, Ellenabeich	Daily 1 April-15 October	10am – 6pm
Appin House, Appin	Daily 13 April – 11 October	10am - 6pm
Ardanaiseig Hotel Gardens	Daily all year	9am - 5pm
Ardchattan Priory, North Connel.	Daily 1 April-31 October	9am – 6pm
Ardkinglas Woodland Garden	Open all year	
Ardmaddy Castle, Balvicar	Daily all year 9am – sunset, or by appt.	
Ascog Hall, Isle of Bute	Daily (except Mon&Tues) mid Apr–mid Oct	
	10am–6pm	
Barguillean's 'Angus Garden'Taynuilt	Open all year	
Cnoc-na-Garrie, Ballymeanoch	First Wednesday, April–October incl. 2 – 6pm	
	or by appointment	
Coille Dharaich, Kilmelford	By appointment April–September	
Crarae Glen Garden, Inveraray	Daily April–October	9am – 6pm
Crinan Hotel Garden, Crinan	Daily 30 April to 30 September	
Dalnaheish, Tayvallich .	April-September by appointment	
Druimavuic House, Appin	Daily 5 April - 29th June	10am – 6pm
Druimneil House, Port Appin	Daily Easter – October	9am – 6pm
Eredine Woodland Garden, Lochaweside	Saturdays all year, except 6 June	11am - 4pm
Jura House, Ardfin, Isle of Jura.	Open all year	9am – 5pm

Kildalloig, Campbeltown .... By appointment
Kinlochlaich House Gardens, Appin. ..... Open all year (except Sundays Oct-Mar)
　　　　　　　　　　　　　　　　　9.30–5.30 or dusk. Suns April-Sept 10.30-5.30.
Mount Stuart, Rothesay, Isle of Bute .... 10–13 April & 1 May–18 Oct, (not Tues & Thurs)
　　　　　　　　　　　　　　　　　House: 11–4.30pm Gardens: 10am-5pm.
Tighnamara, Kilmelford .... By appointment, Spring – Autumn
Torosay Castle Gardens,........................... Open all year
　Isle of Mull .... Summer: 9am-7pm Winter: Sunrise – Sunset

Mount Stuart House & Gardens,
　Isle of Bute .... Easter weekend:10–13 April　10am–5pm
Younger Botanic Garden, Benmore .... Sunday 26 April　　　9.30am – 6pm
Crinan Hotel Garden, Crinan .... Saturday 16 May　　　11am–6pm
Arduaine, Kilmelford .... Sat&Sun 16/17 May　　9.30 – 6pm
Colintraive Gardens Weekend .... Sat&Sun 16/17 May　　2 – 6pm
An Cala, Ellenabeich .... Monday 25 May　　　2 – 6pm
Kyles of Bute Gardens .... Sat&Sun 30 & 31 May　2 – 6pm
Coille Dharaich, Kilmelford . ... Sat&Sun 13/14 June　2 – 6pm
Ardkinglas House, Cairndow .... Sunday 14 June　　　11am - 5pm
Ardchattan Priory Fete .... Sunday 19 July　　　12 – 5pm
Kildalloig, Campbeltown .... Sunday 19 July　　　2 - 5.30pm

ACHNACLOICH, Connel &

(Mrs T E Nelson)
Scottish baronial house by John Starforth of Glasgow. Succession of bulbs, flowering
shrubs, rhododendrons, azaleas and primulas. Woodland garden above Loch Etive.
Plants for sale. Admission by collecting box. Dogs on lead please. On the A85 3 miles
east of Connel.
Admission £1.50   Children free OAPs £1.00
Daily from 6 APRIL to 31st OCTOBER 10am - 6pm
40% between Queen's Nursing Institute (Scotland) and the Gardens Fund of The National Trust
for Scotland

AN CALA, Ellenabeich, Isle of Seil

(Mr & Mrs Thomas Downie)
A small garden of under five acres designed in the 1930s, An Cala sits snugly in its
horse-shoe shelter of surrounding cliffs. A very pretty garden with streams, waterfall,
ponds, many herbaceous plants as well as azaleas, rhododendrons and cherry trees in
spring. Proceed south from Oban on Campbeltown road for 8 miles, turn right at Easdale
sign, a further 8 miles on B844; garden between school and Inshaig Park Hotel.
Admission £1.00 Children free
Daily from 1st APRIL to 15th OCTOBER 10am – 6pm
Donation to Scotland's Gardens Scheme
Special Open Day MONDAY 25th MAY 2 – 6pm
Teas, plants, garden sundries for sale
40% to Kilbrandon Church Windows Fund

APPIN HOUSE, Appin
(Mr & Mrs D Mathieson)
In an elevated position, overlooking the Lynn of Lorne and the islands of Shuna, Lismore and Mull, Appin House has magnificent views. The garden was initially planted in the 1960s. It contains many interesting trees and shrubs, as well as peaceful water features, colourful terraces and borders, and plentiful spring bulbs. The many azaleas make spring time walks particularly fragrant. Dogs on lead please. Plant stall. Off A828 midway between Oban and Fort William. Bus will stop at foot of road.
Admission £1.50   Children free   OAPs £1.00
DAILY 13th APRIL to 11th OCTOBER 10am - 6pm
Donation to Scotland's Gardens Scheme

ARDANAISEIG HOTEL GARDENS, Lochaweside
(Mr Bennie Gray)
Beautifully situated on Lochaweside, Ardanaiseig Country House Hotel is surrounded by some 100 acres of gardens, forest and woodland walks. Primarily a spring garden and originally laid out in the 1820s, there are many varieties of rhododendrons, azaleas, magnolias and other exotic shrubs and specimen trees. An extensive walled garden which has been rather neglected in recent years is being restored to its former standard. Teas. Plant stall. 21 miles from Oban. A85 to junction with B845, follow to Kilchrenan Inn, left to Ardanaiseig.
Admission £2.00 Children 50p
OPEN ALL YEAR 9am - 5pm
Donation to Scotland's Gardens Scheme

ARDCHATTAN PRIORY, North Connel &
(Mrs Sarah Troughton)
Beautifully situated on the north side of Loch Etive. The Priory, founded in 1230, is now a private house. The ruins of the chapel and graveyard, with fine early stones, are in the care of Historic Scotland and open with the garden. The front of the house has a rockery, formal herbaceous and rose borders, with excellent views over Loch Etive. To the west of the house there are shrub borders and a wild garden, numerous roses and over 30 different varieties of Sorbus providing excellent autumn colour. Oban 10 miles. From north, turn left off A828 at Barcaldine on to B845 for 6 miles. From Oban or the east on A85, cross Connel Bridge and turn first right, proceed east on Bonawe road.
Admission £1.50 Children free
Tea and light lunches 11am - 6pm
Daily from 1st APRIL to 31st OCTOBER 9am - 6pm.
A fete will be held on **SUNDAY 19th JULY 12 – 5pm.** .
Donation to Scotland's Gardens Scheme

ARDKINGLAS HOUSE, Cairndow &
(Mr S J Noble)
Set around Ardkinglas House, Robert Lorimer's favourite work, the informal garden of around five acres contains magnificent azaleas, trees and other shrubs. The "Caspian", a large pool, enhances the garden's beauty. Teas, coffee, soft drinks and home baking. Plant stall. Adjacent to Ardkinglas Woodland Gardens. Turn into Cairndow village from A83 Glasgow/Campbeltown road. Enter Ardkinglas estate through iron gates and follow sign.
Admission £1.50 Children free
SUNDAY 14th JUNE 11 am - 5 pm
40% to Ardkinglas Arts Trust

ARDKINGLAS WOODLAND GARDEN, Cairndow ♿ (partly)
(Ardkinglas Estate)
This garden contains one of Britain's finest collections of conifers, including "Europe's Mightiest Conifer" and a spectacular display of rhododendrons. Presently, it is undergoing extensive renovation with many improvements already made. It is hoped that visitors will be interested in seeing the garden develop over the coming years. Picnic facilities. Dogs allowed on lead. Entrance through Cairndow village off A83.
Admission £2.00
OPEN DAILY ALL YEAR ROUND
Donation to Scotland's Gardens Scheme

ARDMADDY CASTLE, Balvicar, by Oban ♿ (mostly)
(Mr & Mrs Charles Struthers)
Ardmaddy Castle, with its woodlands and formal walled garden on one side and extended views to the islands and the sea on the other, has some fine rhododendrons and azaleas with a variety of trees, shrubs, unusual vegetables and flower borders between dwarf box hedges. Woodland walks, recently created water garden. Plant sales area with unusual varieties and vegetables & fruit when available. Oban 13 miles, Easdale 3 miles. 1½ miles of narrow road off B844 to Easdale.
Admission £2.00 Children 50p
DAILY ALL YEAR 9am– sunset
Other visits by arrangement: Tel. 01852 300353
Donations to Scotland's Gardens Scheme

ARDUAINE, Kilmelford ♿
(The National Trust for Scotland)
This outstanding 20-acre garden is situated on a promontory bounded by Loch Melfort and Asknish Bay on the Sound of Jura, and is climatically favoured by the Gulf Stream. It is nationally renowned for rhododendrons, azaleas and magnolias and also has a series of ponds and watercourses and many beautiful herbaceous perennials flowering throughout the season. Located between Oban and Lochgilphead on the A816, sharing an entrance with the Loch Melfort Hotel.
Admission £2.40 Children & OAPs £1.60
SATURDAY & SUNDAY 16th & 17th MAY 9.30 am - 6 pm
40% to The Gardens Fund of The National Trust for Scotland
For other opening details see page 122

 # ASCOG HALL, Ascog, Isle of Bute
(Mr & Mrs W Fyfe)
An attractively landscaped Bateman garden, partly restored after decades of neglect. Narrow paths meander through flower carpeted banks and beds planted with choice perennials and shrubs. The most outstanding feature is a splendid sunken Victorian fernery with glazed roof, a crumbling ruin when the owners' purchased the property in 1986, now fully restored with generous support from Historic Scotland and the Royal Botanic Garden Edinburgh. This rare and beautiful feature houses 80 sub-tropical fern species from all over the world, as well as an ancient Todea barbara, the only surviving fern from the original collection, estimated to be around 1,000 years old. Plant stall. On A886, 3 miles fromWemyss Bay/Rothesay ferry, 11 miles from Colintraive/Rhubodach ferry.
Admission £2.50 Children free, under supervision
OPEN DAILY, except Mondays and Tuesdays, mid APRIL – mid OCTOBER
Donation to Scotland's Gardens Scheme

BARGUILLEAN'S "ANGUS GARDEN", Taynuilt
(Mr Sam Macdonald)
Nine acre woodland garden around eleven acre loch set in the Glen Lonan hills. Spring flowering bulbs, extensive collection of rhododendron hybrids, deciduous azaleas, shrubs, primulas and conifers. Garden recently extended by two acres. Access and car park provided. The garden contains the largest collection of North American rhododendron hybrids in the west of Scotland. Coach tours by arrangement: Tel: 01866 822333 or Fax: 01866 822375. Taynuilt 3 miles.
Admission £2.00 Children free
DAILY ALL YEAR
Donation to Scotland's Gardens Scheme

CNOC-NA-GARRIE, Ballymeanoch, by Lochgilphead
(Mrs Dorothy Thomson)
A garden being created from rough hillside, designed for year-round interest. Large range of alpines, shrubs, grasses, herbaceous plants and bulbs, many grown from seed. Plant stall. 2m south of Kilmartin, A816. Entrance sharp left between cottages and red brick house, continue up track to bungalow.
Admission £1.00 Accompanied children free.
Wednesdays 1st APRIL, 6th MAY, 3rd JUNE, 1st JULY, 5th AUGUST, 2nd SEPTEMBER, 7th OCTOBER 2 – 6pm or by appointment. Tel: 01546 605327.
20% to British Red Cross Society (mid Argyll)   20% to Cancer Relief Macmillan Fund

COILLE DHARAICH, Kilmelford, Oban &
(Drs Alan & Hilary Hill)
Small garden, centred on natural rock outcrop, pool and scree terraces and troughs. Wide variety of primulas, alpines, dwarf conifers, bulbs, bog and small shrubs and plants for wet and windy gardens. No dogs please. Plant stall. Teas. Half a mile from Kilmelford on road signposted "Degnish".
Admission £1.50 Senior citizens £1.00 Children free
SATURDAY & SUNDAY 13th & 14th JUNE 2 - 6 pm
By appointment on most other days from April to September. Tel: 01852 200285
40% to North Argyll Eventide Home Association

COLINTRAIVE GARDENS
Two delightful spring and woodland gardens of varied interest, within easy reach of each other. Set in a scenic corner of Argyll.

1 - **Stronailne**   Mr & Mrs H Andrew

2 - **Dunyvaig**   Mrs M Donald

Please call at No. 1 for admission tickets and directions. Dogs on lead please. Plant stall. On A886, 20 miles from Dunoon.
Admission £1.50 Children 50p includes both gardens
SATURDAY & SUNDAY 16th and 17th MAY 2 - 6 pm
All takings to Scotland's Gardens Scheme

CRARAE, Inveraray 👤 (only Lower Gardens)
(Crarae Gardens Charitable Trust)
Rhododendrons, exotic trees and shrubs in a highland glen. Forest garden opening in 1998. Spectacular spring and autumn colour. Dogs on short lead please. Plant sales and Visitor Centre open April to October. Minard 1 mile. 11 miles south of Inveraray on A83. Admission: Fixed charge. Car parking & children under 5 free
Daily APRIL to OCTOBER 9am - 6pm
Donation to Scotland's Gardens Scheme

CRINAN HOTEL GARDEN, Crinan
(Mr & Mrs N Ryan)
Rock garden with azaleas and rhododendrons created into the hillside over a century ago and sheltered, secluded garden with sloping lawns, unexpected herbaceous beds and spectacular views of the canal and Crinan Loch. Lochgilphead A83. A816 Oban, then A841 Cairnbaan to Crinan. Collecting box.
End APRIL to end SEPTEMBER daily
Special Open Day SATURDAY 16th MAY 11am - 6pm Plant stall. Teas.
Admission £1.50 Accompanied children free
40% to the Leonard Cheshire Foundation

DALNAHEISH, Tayvallich, Carsaig Bay
(Mrs C J Lambie)
Small, informal old garden overlooking the Sound of Jura. Woodland, planted rock, shrubs, bulbs, rhododendrons, azaleas and a wide variety of plants from around the world. Donations. One mile from Tayvallich.
Admission by telephone appointment: Tel. 01546 870286
APRIL to SEPTEMBER
All takings to Scotland's Gardens Scheme

DRUIMAVUIC HOUSE, Appin
(Mr & Mrs Newman Burberry)
Stream, wall and woodland gardens with lovely views over Loch Creran. Spring bulbs, rhododendrons, azaleas, primulas, meconopsis, violas. Dogs on lead please. Plant stall. Route A828 Oban/Fort William, 4 miles south of Appin. Use private road where public signs warn of flooding.
Admission £1.00 Children free
Daily from 5th APRIL to 29th JUNE 10 am - 6 pm
Donation to Scotland's Gardens Scheme

DRUIMNEIL HOUSE, Port Appin
(Mrs J Glaisher & Mr Allan Paterson)
Ten acre garden overlooking Loch Linnhe with many fine varieties of mature trees and rhododendrons and other woodland shrubs. Home made teas available. Two miles from A828. Connel/Fort William road. Sharp left at Airds Hotel, second house on right. Lunches by prior arrangement. Tel: 01631 730228.
Admission £1.00 Children free
Daily from EASTER to OCTOBER 9am – 6pm
All takings to Scotland's Gardens Scheme

EREDINE WOODLAND GARDEN, Lochaweside
(Dr & Mrs K Goel)
Woodland garden of 29 acres consisting of attractive mature trees with abundance of
wild flowers. Rhododendrons, azaleas, cherry trees and many others. Massed
snowdrops followed by daffodils and bluebells. Woodland and lochside walks with
spectacular views. On B840. Ford 8m, Dalmally 20m, Inveraray 23m.
Admission £1.00 Children & OAPs 50p. All children under the age of 12 years must be
accompanied by an adult. No pets allowed (except guide dogs).
OPEN SATURDAYS ALL YEAR (except 6th June) 11am – 4pm
Donation to Scotland's Gardens Scheme

JURA HOUSE, Ardfin, Isle of Jura
(Mr F A Riley-Smith)
Organic walled garden with wide variety of unusual plants and shrubs, including large
Australasian collection. Also interesting woodland and cliff walk, spectacular views.
Points of historical interest, abundant wild life and flowers. Plant stall. Tea tent in
season. Toilet. 5 miles from ferry terminal. Ferries to Islay from Kennacraig by Tarbert:
Admission £2.00 Students £1.00 Children up to 16 free
OPEN ALL YEAR 9 am - 5 pm
Donation to Scotland's Gardens Scheme

KILDALLOIG, Campbeltown & (partially)
(Mr & Mrs Joe Turner)
Coastal garden with some interesting and unusual shrubs and herbaceous perennials.
Woodland walk. Pond area under construction. Teas. Plant stall. Dogs on lead please.
3 miles south of Campbeltown past Davaar Island.
Admission £1.50 Accompanied children free.
SUNDAY 19th JULY 2 - 5.30pm or by appointment. Tel: 01586 553192.
40% to Royal National Lifeboat Institution

KINLOCHLAICH HOUSE GARDENS, Appin & (Gravel paths sloping)
(Mr & Mrs D E Hutchison & Miss F M M Hutchison)
Walled garden, incorporating the West Highlands' largest Nursery Garden Centre.
Display beds of alpines, heathers, primulas, rhododendrons, azaleas and herbaceous
plants. Fruiting and flowering shrubs and trees. Route A828. Oban 23 miles, Fort William
27 miles. Bus stops at gate by Police Station.   Admission £1.50
OPEN DAILY ALL YEAR 9.30am - 5.30pm or dusk except Sundays October to March.
(Sundays April - Sept. 10.30am - 5.30pm)
Donation to Scotland's Gardens Scheme and Appin Village Hall

KYLES OF BUTE SMALL GARDENS, Tighnabruaich
Five small gardens in and around Tighnabruaich within easy reach of each other. Each
garden entirely different with something of interest for everyone. Plant sales. Dogs on
lead please.

1 – **Alt Mhor,** Auchenlochan	Mr & Mrs Peter Scott
2 – **The Cottage,** Tighnabruaich	Col. & Mrs Peter Halliday
3 – **Dunmar,** Tighnabruaich	Mr & Mrs A G Hamilton
4 – **Rhubaan Lodge,** Tighnabruaich	Mr & Mrs R M Scott
5 – **Heatherfield,** Kames	Mr & Mrs David Johnston

Please call at No.1 first for admission tickets and directions.
Admission £1.50 includes all gardens Children 50p
SATURDAY & SUNDAY 30th & 31st MAY 2 – 6pm
All takings to Scotland's Gardens Scheme

MOUNT STUART HOUSE & GARDENS, Rothesay, Isle of Bute &

(Mount Stuart Trust)

Open to the public for the first time in 1995: ancestral home of the Marquesses of Bute; one of Britain's most spectacular High Victorian Gothic houses, set in 300 acres. Fabulous interiors, art collection and architectural detail; extensive grounds with lovely woodland and shoreline walks; exotic gardens, Victorian kitchen garden; mature Victorian pinetum. Tearoom & picnic areas. Pre-booked house/gardens/ranger guided tours available on application. Admission to House & Garden: £6.00 Child £2.50   OAPs £4.50 Family ticket £15. Concessions and group rates given.

Admission to Garden only: £3.50 Child £2 OAPs £.3.00 Family ticket £9.00

House: 11am – 4.30pm Gardens: 10am – 5pm (Last admission to both 4.30pm)

Gardens open **Easter weekend: 10th–13th APRIL and 1st MAY to 18th OCTOBER incl.** Closed Tuesdays and Thursdays. Sorry, guide dogs only.

Donation to Scotland's Gardens Scheme

TIGHNAMARA, Melfort, Kilmelford

(Lt Cmdr & Mrs H D Campbell-Gibson)

This two acre garden set in an ancient oak wood with outstanding views over Loch Melfort has been in the care of one family for 60 years. Fatured in "Country Life" and "Scottish Field", the aim has been to achieve colour and diversity throughout the season. There are paths with terraced beds up the hillside with an interesting variety of shrubs and perennials; a woodland walk with massed rhododendrons leading to a pool surrounded by an extensive range of plants including primulas, hostas, irises, astilbes, cranesbill geraniums and wild flowers; lawns with herbaceous beds and shrubs. One mile from Kilmelford on lochside road to Degnish.

Visitors, either individuals or private parties, are welcome

BY APPOINTMENT from Spring to Autumn. Tel: 01852 200224.

Amission £1.50 Accompanied children free

Donation to Scotland's Gardens Scheme

TOROSAY CASTLE & GARDENS, Isle of Mull

(Mr Christopher James)

Torosay is a beautiful and welcoming family home completed in 1858 by David Bryce in the Scottish Baronial style and is surrounded by 12 acres of spectacular contrasting gardens which include formal terraces, an impressive Italian statue walk, surrounded by varied woodland. Many rare and tender plants. Tearoom. Craft shop. Free parking. Groups welcome. 1½ miles from Craignure. Miniature rail steam/diesel from Craignure. Regular daily ferry service from Oban to Craignure.

Admission to Castle & Gardens £4.50 Children £1.50 Concessions £3.50

Castle open Easter weekend - mid October 10.30am - 5.30pm

GARDENS OPEN ALL YEAR Summer 9am - 7pm; Winter sunrise - sunset, with reduced admission when Castle closed.

Donation to Scotland's Gardens Scheme

YOUNGER BOTANIC GARDEN, Benmore   ♿ (limited due to hill slopes)
(Specialist Garden of the Royal Botanic Garden, Edinburgh)
World famous for its magnificent conifers and its extensive range of flowering trees and
shrubs, including over 250 species of rhododendron. From a spectacular avenue of Giant
Redwoods, numerous waymarked walks lead the visitor via a formal garden and pond
through hillside woodlands to a dramatic viewpoint overlooking the Eachaig valley and
the Holy Loch. James Duncan Cafe (licensed) and Botanics Shop for gifts and plants.
Dogs permitted on a short leash. 7m north of Dunoon or 22m south from Glen Kinglass
below Rest and Be Thankful pass; on A815.
Admission £3.00 Concessions £2.50 Children £1.00 Families £7.00
SUNDAY 26th APRIL   9.30am – 6pm
40% to Royal Botanic Garden Edinburgh

AYRSHIRE

District Organiser:	**The Countess of Lindsey**, Gilmilnscroft, Sorn, Mauchline KA5 6ND
Area Organisers:	**Mrs R F Cuninghame,** Caprington Castle, Kilmarnock KA2 9AA
	Mrs John Greenall, Lagg House, Dunure KA7 4LE
	Mrs R Y Henderson, Blairston, by Ayr KA7 4EF
	Mrs R M Yeomans, Ashcraig, Skelmorlie PA17 5HB
Hon. Treasurer:	**Mrs Edith Kerr,** Bank of Scotland, 123 High Street, Ayr KA7 1QP

DATES OF OPENING

Bargany, Girvan	1 March - 31 Oct	10am - 7pm or dusk
Blair, Dalry	All year round	
Culzean Castle & Country Park	Sunday 19 April	10.30am – 5pm
Culzean Castle & Country Park	Sunday 3 May	10.30am – 5pm
Beoch, Maybole	Sunday 10 May	2 – 5pm
Auchincruive, Ayr	Sunday 17 May	1 – 5.30pm
Ashcraig, Skelmorlie	Sunday 24 May	2 – 5.30pm
Doonholm, Ayr	Sunday 7 June	2 – 5.30pm
Symington Village	Sunday 21 June	2 – 5pm
Knockdolian, Colmonell	Sunday 28 June	2 – 5.30pm
Barnweil, Craigie, nr Kilmarnock	Sunday 5 July	2 – 5pm
Penkill Castle, near Girvan	Sunday 12 July	2 - 5pm
Culzean Castle & Country Park	Sunday 19 July	10.30am – 5pm
Barr Village	Sat/Sun 25 & 26 July	1 – 5pm
Carnell, Hurlford	Sunday 26 July	2 – 5.30pm
Skeldon, Dalrymple	Sunday 2 August	2 – 6pm
Blairquhan, Straiton, Maybole	Sunday 16 August	1.30 – 4.30pm

ASHCRAIG, Skelmorlie
(Mr & Mrs Richard Yeomans)
Garden originally laid out in 1820, consisting of lawns, woodland and formal gardens, walled garden, also informal cottage garden. Many interesting trees and shrubs including large collection of rhododendrons, azaleas and hydrangeas. Plant stall. Tea and biscuits. Cars free. On A78 4 miles north of Largs, approx. 1½ miles south of Skelmorlie.
Admission £2.00 Children 50p
SUNDAY 24th MAY 2 – 5.30pm
40% to Cancer Research Campaign (Scotland)

AUCHINCRUIVE, Ayr &
(Scottish Agricultural College)
Classical house of 1764-67 built for the Oswald family. Interior decoration by Robert Adam. Extensive amenity grounds of the College campus, the setting for buildings and other facilities serving all aspects of the educational, research and consultancy work of the college. Attractive riverside gardens with plant display, herbaceous and shrub borders; arboretum; a range of outdoor and protected commercial crops at Mansionfield Unit, together forming part of a horticultural teaching & research department. Features include Farm Walk and Vintage Vehicle Display. Disabled facilities. Car parking free. Afternoon Tea in Refectory. Wide selection of pot plants, shrubs & Auchincruive honey for sale. Ayr 3m. Route B743. Ayr to Annbank & Tarbolton buses stop at College gate.
Admission £3.00 Children under 14 free Senior Citizens £1.50
SUNDAY 17th MAY 1 - 5.30 pm
40% between Erskine Hospital, the Scottish War Blind and the British Red Cross Society

BARGANY, Girvan &
(N J F Dalrymple Hamilton)
This woodland garden has a lily pond with island, surrounded by masses of yellow, pink and white azaleas, and a huge variety of species rhododendron flowering from April to June. In conjunction with many fine hard and softwood trees, there is a small rock garden and spring displays of daffodils and snowdrops, and autumn colours. Plant stall. Route: take B734 from Girvan towards Dailly, four miles on left.
Admission: Contribution box
1st MARCH – 31st OCTOBER 10am–7pm or dusk
Donation to Scotland's Gardens Scheme

BARNWEIL, Craigie, near Kilmarnock &
(Mr & Mrs Ronald Alexander)
A garden which has been developed from scratch during the last 20 years. Formally planned and colour co-ordinated herbaceous and some shrub rose borders surround the house. These give way to the woodland garden which features rhododendrons, azaleas, ferns, meconopsis and primulas, as well as a golden border. Other features of the garden are beech, and mixed beech and holly hedges, which provide much needed shelter on this rather exposed site. On a clear day, there are fine views to the north for 60-70 miles to Ben Lomond and beyond. Home baked teas. Cars free. Craigie 2 miles. Route: right off B730, 2 miles south of A77.
Admission £1.50 Children under 12 free
SUNDAY 5th JULY 2 - 5 pm
40% to Tarbolton Parish Church

BARR VILLAGE GARDENS   &

A large number of attractive gardens, some old, some new, within this small and beautiful conservation village. Maps and tickets available at each open garden. Teas in Barr CommunityHall. Plant stall. Large nursery garden on outskirts of village. Barr is on B734, Girvan 8 miles, Ballantrae 17 miles, Ayr 24 miles.
Admission £1.50 Children under 12 50p
SATURDAY & SUNDAY 25th & 26th JULY 1 – 5pm
40% to Childrens Hospice Association Scotland

BEOCH, Maybole

(Lord Maclehose)
A wooded glen with burn and bluebells leads up to Beoch on the Carrick hills. Unusual and well chosen ornamental trees, shrubs and underplanting enhance this smaller garden situated on the open hillside with wide panoramic views inland. Tea and biscuits. Some plants for sale. Maybole 3½ miles. Take the High Road B7024 from Ayr to Maybole, turn right after Culroy. Garden signposted thereafter.
Admission £1.50 Children under 14 free
SUNDAY 10th MAY 2 – 5pm
40% to Riding for the Disabled Association (Carrick Group)

BLAIR, Dalry

(Mrs M G Borwick)
The extensive and fine-timbered policies surrounding this tower house of great antiquity, are first mentioned by Pont in the early 17th century. The well laid out park is attributed to Captain William Fordyce Blair RN in the 1850s. Visitors are permitted to walk through these delightful historic grounds all the year round and will find much to admire and enjoy. Route: from A737 in Dalry go to railway station. Entrance ½ mile beyond station.
OPEN ALL YEAR
Donations to Scotland's Gardens Scheme. Ask at house.

BLAIRQUHAN, Straiton, Maybole &

(Mr James Hunter Blair)
Castle in Tudor style designed by William Burn, 1820-24 for Sir David Hunter Blair, 3rd Bart. Sixty-foot high saloon with gallery. The kitchen courtyard is formed with stones and sculpture from an earlier castle. All the original furniture made for the house is still in it. There is a good collection of pictures and a gallery of paintings by the Scottish Colourists. Three mile private drive along the River Girvan. Walled garden with herbaceous border and Regency glasshouse. The Castle is surrounded by an extensive park including an arboretum. Admission price includes tour of house. Tea in house. One mile west of Straiton. Entry from B7045.
Admission £3.50 Children £2.00 OAPs £2.50
SUNDAY 16th AUGUST 1.30 – 4.30 pm
20% to Kyle & Carrick Civic Society   20% to Leonard Cheshire Fund in Scotland

CARNELL, Hurlford ♿
(Mr & Mrs J R Findlay)
Alterations in 1843 by William Burn. 16th century peel tower. Walled garden, rock and water gardens; 100 yards herbaceous border and new 100 yard phlox and shrub border. Herbaceous borders around Carnell House with extensive Plant Sale. Home baking stall. Silver band. Ice cream and cream teas. Cars free. Kilmarnock 6 miles. Mauchline 4 miles on A76. 1½ miles on Ayr side of A719.
Admission £2.00 School children free
SUNDAY 26th JULY 2 - 5.30pm
40% between Craigie Parish Church & Craigie Village Hall, Hansel Village, the British Red Cross Society and Marie Curie Cancer Care

---

CULZEAN CASTLE & COUNTRY PARK, Maybole ♿
(The National Trust for Scotland)
This is the Trust's most visited garden property. The Fountain Garden lies in front of Robert Adam's magnificent castle, with terraces and herbaceous borders reflecting its Georgian elegance. Scotland's first Country Park, consisting of 563 acres, contains a wealth of interest from shoreline through Deer Park and Swan Pond to mature parklands, gardens, woodland walks and adventure playground. A conservatory has been restored to its former glory as an orangery, and recent restorations include the Ruined Arch, Viaduct, Ice House, a unique Pagoda and the beautiful Camellia House. Visitor Centre & Restaurants, ranger-led excursions. Route: A719, Maybole 4 miles. Combined ticket for Castle & Country Park: £6.50/£4.40. Family £17. Country Park only: £3.50/£2.40 Family £9.
Open 1 April – 31 October 10.30am–5pm.
Scotland's Garden Scheme Tours 2 – 3.30pm on:
SUNDAYS 19th APRIL, 3rd MAY & 19th JULY.
Tours start at ruined arch by Deer Park car park.
40% to The Gardens Fund of The National Trust for Scotland
For other opening details see page 125

DOONHOLM, Ayr ♿ (limited)
(Mr Peter Kennedy)
Informal gardens in attractive setting on the banks of the River Doon. Mature trees, shrubs and marvellous show of rhododendrons and azaleas. Tea and biscuits. Plant stall. Signposted from Burns Cottage, Alloway and from A77.
Admission £2.00 Children & OAPs £1.00
SUNDAY 7th JUNE 2 – 5.30pm
40% between Multiple Sclerosis Society and Cancer Relief Macmillan Fund

---

 # KNOCKDOLIAN, Colmonell ♿ (partly)
(The Duchess of Wellington)
1¼ acre walled garden, extensive range of shrubs, herbaceous and rockery. Greenhouses including vinery. Classical peach case. Remains of fortified house built c1620 for the Kennedy and McCubbin family. Extensive policies with river walks. Teas and home baking. Large plant stall. 1½ miles from Colmonell, 3½ miles from Ballantrae on junction of B734 and B7044.
Admission £2.00 Children under 16 free
SUNDAY 28th JUNE 2 – 5.30pm
40% to Colmonell Parish Church

PENKILL CASTLE, near Girvan   ♿ (limited)
(Mr & Mrs Patrick Dromgoole)
A series of three Victorian gardens, vegetable, formal and landscaped, linked by a "wild walk" overlooking a burn leading to the Penwhapple river. Currently undergoing restoration work by the present owners. Teas. Plant and other stalls, bagpipes, Scottish dancing. Route: 3 miles east of Girvan on Old Dailly to Barr road.
Admission £2.00 Children under 12 free
SUNDAY 12th JULY 2 - 5pm
40% to Barr Parish Church

SKELDON, Dalrymple
(Mr S E Brodie QC & Mrs Brodie)
One and a half acres of formal garden with herbaceous borders and arched pathways. Large Victorian glasshouse with a substantial collection of plants and four acres of woodland garden within a unique setting on the banks of the River Doon. Home baked teas. Silver band on the lawn. Plants for sale. Cars free. Dalrymple, B7034 between Dalrymple and Hollybush.
Admission £2.00 Children & OAPs £1.00
SUNDAY 2nd AUGUST 2 - 6 pm
40% between The Mental Health Foundation and Marie Curie Cancer Care

---

 # SYMINGTON VILLAGE   ♿ (partly)
Symington is a beautiful conservation village with its attractive houses and a unique Parish Church dating from the 12th century. Several of its garden owners have agreed to open to the public for the first time. Each with a distinctive character, the gardens feature a wide variety of shrubs, trees, alpines, heathers and herbaceous plants, all within 10 minutes walking distance of the Church. Home baked teas. Plant stall. Dogs on leads please. Signposted on A77, 5 miles south of Kilmarnock. Plans and tickets from Church Hall, Main Street, adjacent to Church.
Admission £2.00 OAPs £1.50 Accompanied children free
SUNDAY 21st JUNE 2 – 5pm
40% to Symington Parish Church

BERWICKSHIRE

District Organiser:	**Col S J Furness,** The Garden House, Netherbyres, Eyemouth TD14 5SE
Area Organisers:	**The Hon Mrs Charles Ramsay,** Bughtrig, Leitholm, Coldstream TD14 4JP
	Miss Jean Thomson, Stable Cottage, Lambden, Greenlaw, Duns TD10 6UN
Hon. Treasurer:	**Mr Richard Melvin**, Bank of Scotland, 88 High Street, Coldstream TD12 4AQ

DATES OF OPENING

Bughtrig, Leitholm .... June– September 11am – 5pm, or by appointment
The Hirsel, Coldstream .... Open daily all year, reasonable daylight hours
Manderston, Duns .... Sundays & Thursdays 14 May – 27 September

Netherbyres, Eyemouth .... Sunday 19 April	2 - 6pm
Manderston, Duns .... Monday 25 May	2-5.30pm
Whitchester House, Duns .... Sunday 31 May	2 - 5.30pm
Charterhall, Duns .... Sunday 24 May	2 - 5pm
Shannobank, Abbey St Bathans .... Sunday 12 July	2 - 5pm
Netherbyres, Eyemouth .... Sunday 19 July	2 - 6pm
Manderston, Duns .... Monday 31 August	2-5.30pm

BUGHTRIG, Near Leitholm, Coldstream ♿ (mainly)
(Major General & The Hon Mrs Charles Ramsay)
A traditional, hedged Scottish family garden, with an interesting combination of
herbaceous plants, shrubs, annuals, vegetables and fruit. It is surrounded by fine
specimen trees which provide remarkable shelter. Small picnic area. Parking. Special
arrangements for bona fide groups. Accommodation in house possible for 4–8 guests.
Half mile east of Leitholm on B6461.
Admission £1.50 OAPs £1.00 Children 50p
Open daily JUNE to SEPTEMBER 11am-5pm or by appt: 01890 840678
Donation to Scotland's Gardens Scheme

CHARTERHALL, Duns ♿
(Mr & Mrs Alexander Trotter)
Hybrid rhododendrons and
azaleas in mature grounds.
Flower garden, surrounding
modern house. Small greenhouse
and vegetable garden. Tea with
home bakes and biscuits. Plant
stall.
6 miles south west of Duns and 3
miles east of Greenlaw on B6460.
Admission £2.00 Children £1.00
SUNDAY 24th MAY 2 - 5 pm
40% to Scottish Dyslexia Trust

THE HIRSEL, Coldstream ᒻ (mainly)
(The Earl of Home CVO CBE)
Snowdrops and aconites in Spring; daffodils in March/April; rhododendrons and azaleas in late May/early June, and magnificent autumn colouring. Walks round the lake, Dundock Wood and Leet valley. Marvellous old trees. Dogs on leads, please. Homestead Museum, Craft Centre and Workshops. Tearoom (parties please book). Immediately west of Coldstream on A697. Parking charge only.
OPEN DAILY ALL YEAR (Reasonable daylight hours)
Donation to Scotland's Gardens Scheme

MANDERSTON, Duns ᒻ
(The Lord Palmer)
The swan song of the great classical house. Formal and woodland gardens. Tearoom in grounds. 2 miles east of Duns on A6105. Buses from Galashiels and Berwick. Alight at entrance on A6105.
Admission: Prices unavailable at time of going to press.
SUNDAYS & THURSDAYS 14th MAY to 27th SEPTEMBER,
HOLIDAY MONDAYS 25th MAY and 31st AUGUST 2 - 5.30 pm
Parties any time by appointment. Tel: 01361 883450
Donation to Scotland's Gardens Scheme

NETHERBYRES, Eyemouth ᒻ
(Col S J Furness & GRBS)
Unique 18th century elliptical walled garden, with a new house built inside. Daffodils and wild flowers in the spring. Annuals, roses, herbaceous borders and coloured borders during the summer. Produce stall. Teas in house. Eyemouth ¼ mile on A1107.
Admission £2.00 Children £1.00
SUNDAY 19th APRIL 2 - 6 pm   *40% to Marie Curie Cancer Care*
SUNDAY 19th JULY 2 - 6 pm   *40% to Royal National Rose Society*
Also by appointment for parties of 10 or more. Tel: 01890 750337

SHANNOBANK, Abbey St Bathans
(Mr John Dobie)
A new garden created in the last 10 years on an exposed site surrounding a farmhouse and outbuildings with superb views. A mixture of fruit, ornamental trees, shrub roses, hardy shrubs and perennials. Woodland walks. Teas available in house and at Riverside Restaurant, Abbey St Bathans. Cake and plant stalls. Half mile north west of Abbey St Bathans between Duns (7m) and Grantshouse signposted on A6112 and B6355.
Admission £1.50
SUNDAY 12th JULY 2 - 5pm
40% to Abbey St Bathans Village Hall Fund

WHITCHESTER HOUSE, Duns ᒻ
(Kings Bible College)
Rhododendrons and azaleas. Walled garden. A once famous garden which the owners are trying hard to restore with their own labour. Teas. Duns 7 miles, off B6355.
Admission £1.50 Children free
SUNDAY 31st MAY 2 - 5.30pm
40% to Kings Bible College

CAITHNESS & SUTHERLAND

Joint District Organisers: **Mrs Robert Howden,** The Firs, Langwell, Berriedale, Caithness KW7 6HD

Mrs Colin Farley-Sutton, Shepherd's Cottage, Watten, Caithness KW1 5YJ

Area Organiser: **Mrs Richard Tyser,** Gordonbush, Brora KW9 6LX

Hon. Treasurer: **Mr George MacDonald,** Clydesdale Bank, 17 Traill Street, Thurso KW14 7EL

DATES OF OPENING

Dunrobin Castle, Golspie	Saturday 20 June	10.30am – 5.30pm
Castle of Mey	Wednesday 22 July	2 – 6pm
Sandside House, Reay	Sunday 26 July	2 – 5pm
Castle of Mey	Thursday 30 July	2 – 6pm
House of Tongue, Tongue	Saturday 1 August	2 – 6pm
Langwell, Berriedale	Sunday 9 August	2 – 6pm
Langwell, Berriedale	Sunday 16 August	2 – 6pm
Dunbeath Castle, Dunbeath	Sunday 23 August	2 - 6pm
Castle of Mey	Saturday 5 September	2 – 6pm

CASTLE OF MEY, Mey, Caithness &
(H.M. Queen Elizabeth The Queen Mother)
Z-plan castle formerly the seat of the Earls of Caithness. 18th and 19th century additions.
Remodelled 1954. Old walled-in garden. On north coast and facing the Pentland Firth
and Orkney. Cars free. Teas served under cover. Mey 1½ mile. Route A836. Bus: Please
enquire at local bus depots. Special buses can be arranged.
Admission £2.00 Children under 12 free OAPs £1.00
WEDNESDAY 22nd JULY 2 - 6pm
40% to Scottish Disability Foundation (Edinburgh)
THURSDAY 30th JULY and SATURDAY 5th SEPTEMBER 2 - 6pm
40% to Queen's Nursing Institute (Scotland)

DUNBEATH CASTLE, Dunbeath &
(Mr & Mrs S W Murray Threipland)
Traditional walled garden recently re-landscaped and containing magnificent display of
herbaceous and greenhouse plants, together with vegetable garden and heather corner.
Short woodland walk. Teas served in former coach house. Route: A9 to Dunbeath
village Post Office, then follow old A9 south for 1¼ miles to castle gates.
Admission £1.50 Children under 12 and OAPs £1.00
SUNDAY 23rd AUGUST 2 - 6pm
40% to Childrens Hospice Association Scotland

DUNROBIN CASTLE & GARDENS, Golspie

(The Sutherland Trust)

Formal gardens laid out in 1850 by the architect, Barry. Set beneath the fairytale castle of Dunrobin. Tearoom and gift shop in castle. Picnic site and woodland walks. Dunrobin Castle Museum in the gardens. Suitable for disabled by prior arrangement.

Group admission: Adults £4.50, children & OAPs £3.00, family £15.00. Castle one mile north of Golspie on A9.

Admission £5.00 Children & OAPs £3.50

SATURDAY 20th JUNE 10.30 am - 5.30 pm. (Last admission 5 pm)

40% to the British Lung Foundation

HOUSE OF TONGUE, Tongue, Lairg ♿ (partially)

(The Countess of Sutherland)

17th century house on Kyle of Tongue. Walled garden, herbaceous borders, old fasioned roses. Teas available at the Ben Loyal and Tongue Hotels. Tongue half a mile. House just off main road approaching causeway.

Admission to garden £1.50 Children 50p

SATURDAY 1st AUGUST 2 - 6 pm

40% to Children First

LANGWELL, Berriedale ♿

(The Lady Anne Bentinck)

A beautiful old walled-in garden situated in the secluded Langwell strath. Charming access drive with a chance to see deer. Cars free. Teas served under cover. Berriedale 2 miles. Route A9.

Admission £1.50 Children under 12 & OAPs £1.00

SUNDAY 9th AUGUST and SUNDAY 16th AUGUST 2 - 6 pm

40% to Royal National Lifeboat Institution

SANDSIDE HOUSE GARDENS by Reay, Thurso ♿ (partially)

(Mr & Mrs Geoffrey Minter)

Old walled gardens being restored but well stocked. Sunken rectangular walled garden. Upper garden with sea views to the Orkneys and Grade A listed 2-seater privy. Terrace with rockery overlooking sunken garden. Main gate is on A836 half mile west of Reay village. Teas. There is a splayed entrance with railings and gate lodge.

Admission £1.50 Children under 12 £1.00

SUNDAY 26th JULY 2 - 5pm

40% to The Highland Hospice

> *SGS runs an annual six-day coach tour,*
> *visiting two or three gardens each day*
> *and based in a comfortable hotel for five nights.*
> *The tour starts and ends in Edinburgh —*
> *ask us for a brochure in December*

CLYDESDALE

District Organiser:	**Mrs J S Mackenzie,** The Old Manse, Elsrickle, Lanarkshire ML12 6QZ
Area Organiser:	**Mr Charles Brandon,** Cherry Tree Cottage, 2 Glenburn Avenue, Symington ML12 6LH
Hon. Treasurer:	**Mr M J Prime,** Elmsleigh, Broughton Road, Biggar, Lanarkshire ML12 6AM

DATES OF OPENING

Baitlaws, Lamington .... July – August by appointment
Biggar Park, Biggar .... By appointment

Carmichael Mill, Hyndford Bridge .... Sunday 19 April	10am–5pm
Edmonston House, Biggar .... Sunday 7 June	2 – 6pm
Dippoolbank Cottage, Carnwath .... Sunday 14 June	2 – 6pm
Carmichael Mill, Hyndford Bridge .... Sunday 5 July	2 – 5pm
Biggar Park, Biggar .... Sunday 19 July	2 – 6pm
Dippoolbank Cottage, Carnwath .... Sunday 19 July	2 – 6pm
Baitlaws, Lamington .... Sunday 26 July	2 – 5pm
Roberton Garden Trail .... Sunday 9 August	2 – 5pm
Culter Allers, Coulter .... Sunday 16 August	2 – 6pm

BAITLAWS, Lamington, Biggar
(Mr & Mrs M Maxwell Stuart)
As seen on 'The Beechgrove Garden' in October 1997, the garden has been developed over the past eighteen years with a particular emphasis on colour combinations of hardy shrubs and herbaceous plants, many unusual. Set at around 900 ft above sea level, there are magnificent views of the surrounding hills. Large and varied plant stall. Teas. Route: off A702 above Lamington village. Biggar 5 miles, Abington 5 miles, Lanark 10 miles.
Admission £2.00 Children over 12 25p
SUNDAY 26th JULY 2 - 5 pm and by appointment JULY & AUGUST Tel: 01899 850240
40% to Biggar Museum Trust

BIGGAR PARK, Biggar   ⅙ (partially)
(Mr & Mrs David Barnes)
Ten acre garden, starred in the 1998 Good Gardens Guide, incorporating traditional walled garden with long stretches of herbaceous borders and shrubberies as well as fruit, vegetables and greenhouses. Lawns, walks, pools and many other interesting features. Good collection of shrub roses in July. Many interesting young trees. Home made teas and plants for sale on open day. On A702, quarter mile south of Biggar.
Admission £2.00 Children 50p. Groups welcome by appointment. Tel: 01899 220185.
SUNDAY 19th JULY 2 – 6pm
40% to Multiple Sclerosis Society

CARMICHAEL MILL, Hyndford Bridge, Lanark & (partially)
(Chris & Ken Fawell)
Riverside gardens surrounding the only remaining workable water powered grain mill
on the River Clyde a few miles upstream from the New Lanark Heritage textile mills.
Grain mill working, river levels permitting. Informal and wild gardens with riverside
walks, herbaceous and shrubberies, fruit and vegetables. Over 200 different ornamental
trees. Also to be seen in the grounds evidence of the use of water power back to
medieval times including grain mills, foundry, lint mill, threshing mill. Plant stall. Teas.
Admission to gardens and mill £3.00 Children over 12 £1.00 OAPs £2.00
SUNDAY 19th APRIL 10am – 5pm. Spring flowering trees and daffodils.
In conjunction with Mill Awareness Day. Archaeologists on site to explain.
40% to Biggar Museum Archaelogists Section
SUNDAY 5th JULY 2 - 5pm Gardens at summer peak.
Friends of Lanark Museum Trust on sites.
40% to The Royal Burgh of Lanark Museum Trust

CULTER ALLERS, Coulter & (partially)
(The McCosh Family)
Culter Allers, a late Victorian gothic house, maintained its traditional one acre walled
kitchen garden which continues to provide vegetables, fruit and flowers for the family.
Peas and sweet peas, potatoes and poppies, cabbages and cornflowers, are bordered by
box hedges. Areas of the kitchen garden have been opened out into lawn, a formal rose
garden around a well, a herb garden and herbaceous borders. The remainder of the
grounds are open and include a woodland walk, an avenue of 125 year old lime trees
leading to the village church and a croquet lawn for those needing moderate exercise.
Weather permitting, some classic vehicles will be on view. Teas and a plant stall. In the
village of Coulter, 3 miles south of Biggar on A702.
Admission £1.50 Children free
SUNDAY 16th AUGUST 2 - 6 pm
20% to Coulter Library Trust 20% to Marie Curie Cancer Care

DIPPOOLBANK COTTAGE, Carnwath
(Mr Allan Brash & children)
Artist's intriguing cottage garden. Vegetables grown in small beds. Herbs, fruit, flowers.
Garden now extended to include pond, with flowers, trees, etc. Route: off B7016, 2½m
Carnwath, 3m Auchengray Church Hall. Well signed.
SUNDAYS 14th JUNE and 19th JULY 2 - 6pm
40% to Cancer Relief Macmillan Fund

EDMONSTON HOUSE, Biggar & (partially)
(Mr & Mrs H A Whitson)
Grounds with late spring flowers, greenhouse, lake and waterfall. Woodland walk.
Home baked teas in house. Plant stall. Edinburgh/Dumfries buses stop at Candy Mill
on A702, ½ mile from garden.
Admission £1.50 Children free
SUNDAY 7th JUNE 2 – 6pm
40% to Dunsyre Holiday Camp

#ROBERTON GARDEN TRAIL ♿ (some)
The gardens are all different and include herbaceous, shrubs and conifer beds, plus a
wild garden and an alpine house. Teas in Village Hall. Plant stall. Roberton is on the
A73, 9 miles from Biggar and 14 miles from Lanark.
NB Visitors must use the car park, unless disabled.
Admission £2.00 includes all open gardens Children 50p
SUNDAY 9th AUGUST 2 – 5pm
40% to Glencaple Parish Church

DUMFRIES

District Organiser & Hon Treasurer:	**Mrs Alison Graham,** Peilton, Moniaive, Thornhill DG3 4HE
Area Organisers:	**Mr W Carson,** 53 Castledykes Road, Dumfries DG1 4SN
	Mrs M Johnson-Ferguson, Springkell, Eaglesfield DG11 3AL
	Mrs Allen Paterson, Grovehill, Thornhill DG3 4HD

DATES OF OPENING

Arbigland, Kirkbean	Tuesdays to Sundays: May - September Also Bank Holiday Mondays	2 – 6pm
The Crichton, Dumfries	Sunday 17 May	2 – 5pm
Dalswinton, Auldgirth	Sunday 31 May	2 – 5pm
Drumpark, Dunscore	Sunday 7 June	2 – 5pm
Drumclyer, Irongray	Sunday 14 June	2 – 5pm
Craigielands Mill, Beattock	Sunday 21 June	2 – 5pm
The Garth, Tynron	Sunday 21 June	2 – 5pm
Skairfield, Lockerbie	Sunday 28 June	2 – 5pm
Kirkland, Courance	Sunday 5 July	2 – 5pm

ARBIGLAND, Kirkbean
(Captain & Mrs J B Blackett)
Woodland, formal and water gardens arranged round a secluded bay. The garden where
Admiral John Paul Jones worked as a boy in the 18th century. Cars free. Picnic area by
sandy beach. Dogs on lead, please. Home baked tea in rustic tea room. Signposted on
A710 Solway Coast Road.
Admission £2.00 Children over 5 50p OAPs £1.50
TUESDAYS TO SUNDAYS: MAY - SEPTEMBER 2 - 6 pm
ALSO BANK HOLIDAY MONDAYS. House open 22nd – 31st May.
Donation to Scotland's Gardens Scheme and SSAFA

CRAIGIELANDS MILL, Beattock ♿
(Mr & Mrs Michael Henry)
Informal woodland garden created ten years ago in grounds of converted sawmill. Pond with ornamental ducks. Mill stream. Teas. Sorry no dogs. Route: off A74 into Beattock village. Follow A701 under railway bridge and immediately right.
Admission £2.00
SUNDAY 21st JUNE 2 – 5pm
40% to Cancer Relief Macmillan Fund

THE CRICHTON, Dumfries
(Crichton Development Company)
Beautiful and extensive grounds of some 34 hectares, landscaped with mature rhododendrons, azaleas and many specimen trees, including Davidia involucrata (handkerchief tree) and Liriodendron tulipifera (tulip tree). Large rock garden complete with waterfall, ornamental pond and bog garden. The Crichton Memorial Church, an imposing red sandstone building, is a hundred years old and there are many other listed buildings, including Easterbrook Hall. Many events on the day. Teas at Easterbrook Hall. Route: B725, Dumfries 1 mile.
Admission £2.00 Accompanied children £1.00 Cars free
SUNDAY 17th MAY 2 - 5 pm
40% to Crichton Royal Amenity Fund

DALSWINTON HOUSE, Auldgirth
(Sir David & Lady Landale)
Woodland and lochside walks. Cake and plant stall. Home baked teas. Dumfries 7 miles. Dumfries/Auldgirth bus via Kirkton stops at lodge.
Admission £2.00
SUNDAY 31st MAY 2 - 5pm
40% to Kirkmahoe Parish Church

DRUMCLYER, Irongray, by Dumfries ♿
(Mrs Jill Hardy)
Rhododendrons and azaleas. Small woodland garden and walled garden. Teas. Plant stall. Between Shawhead and the Rouken Bridge.
Admission £2.00 Children 50p
SUNDAY 14th JUNE 2 – 5pm
40% to Dumfries Choral Society

DRUMPARK, Dunscore
(Mrs Maurice Mitchell)
The garden is situated round the new house built 20 years ago, the old one having been completely demolished. In the spring and early summer rhododendrons, especially small ones, and other flowering shrubs are the main features, with primulas, meconopsis and bulbs growing among them. There is also a water garden and a wild garden. Tea. Plant stall. Dunscore 3½ miles. Dumfries 7 miles. Shawhead 3 miles.
Admission £2.00 Children 50p Cars free
SUNDAY 7th JUNE 2 – 5pm
40% to Irongray Parish Church

The GARTH, Tynron
(Mimi Craig & Jock Harkness)
Old manse, established 1750 with additions. 2 acre garden, woodland, waterside and walled garden. The walled garden is being reconstructed and much heavy maintenance has been achieved throughout. Teas in Tynron Village Hall. Route: off A702 between Penpont and Moniaive.
Admission £1.75
SUNDAY 21st JUNE 2 - 5pm
40% to Village Hall Fund

KIRKLAND, Courance
(Mr & Mrs R M Graham)
Walled garden. New rock garden. Natural woodland gardens with ponds and young trees on a conservation theme. Teas. Route: A701 1½ miles north of Parkgate. Halfway between Moffat and Dumfries. Parking in farmyard.
Admission £2.00
SUNDAY 5th JULY 2 – 5pm
40% to Marie Curie Cancer Care

SKAIRFIELD, Hightae, Lockerbie &
(Mrs M F Jardine Paterson)
Walled garden with herbaceous, fruit and vegetables. Shrubs. Teas under cover. Plant stall. Signed off B7020 between Lochmaben and Dalton.
Admission £2.00 Children 50p OAPs £1.00
SUNDAY 28th JUNE 2 – 5pm
40% to Cancer Research

DUNBARTONSHIRE WEST

District Organiser:	**Mrs T C Duggan,** Kirkton Cottage, Darleith Road, Cardross G82 5EZ
Area Organisers:	**Mrs James Dykes,** Dawn, 42 East Abercromby Street, Helensburgh G84 9JA
	Mrs R C Hughes, Brambletye, Argyll Road, Kilcreggan, G84 0JY
	Mrs J S Lang, Ardchapel, Shandon, Helensburgh G84 8NP
	Mrs W A C Reynolds, North Stanley Lodge, Cove, Helensburgh G84 0NY
	Mrs H G Thomson, 47 Campbell St., Helensburgh G84 9QW
Hon. Treasurer:	**Dr D P Braid,** 41 Charlotte Street, Helensburgh G84 7SE

DATES OF OPENING

Auchendarroch, Tarbet .... 1 April-31 August by appointment
Glenarn, Rhu .... Daily 21 March–21 September, sunrise–sunset

Glenarn, Rhu .... Sunday 3 May   2–5.30pm
Auchendarroch, Tarbet .... Sunday 10 May   2–5.30pm
The Linn Garden, Cove .... Sunday 17 May   2 – 6pm
Shandon Gardens .... Sunday 24 May   2–5.30pm
Geilston House, Cardross .... Saturday 30 May   2–5.30pm
Ross Priory, Gartocharn .... Sunday 31 May   2 – 6pm
Cardross Gardens .... Sunday 7 June   2 - 5pm
Geilston House, Cardross .... Sunday 19 July   2–5.30pm
The Hill House Plant Sale, Helensburgh .... Sunday 6 September   11am–5pm

AUCHENDARROCH, Tarbet
(Mrs Hannah Stirling)
Five acre garden, superbly set on shores of Loch Lomond. Wild garden, woodland walk, wide range of heathers, flowering trees and shrubs including cherries, rhododendrons and azaleas and, in due season, a new bed of 72 yellow roses gifted to Mrs Stirling by David Austin. Regal pelargoniums particularly notable. Plant stall. Dogs on lead only. Immediately south of Tarbet on A82, lower entrance gate beside Tarbet Pier.
SUNDAY 10th MAY 2 - 5.30pm   Tea and shortbread. Admission £1.50 Children free
1st APRIL to 31st AUGUST by appointment. Tel. 01301 702240
40% to Friends of Loch Lomond

CARDROSS GARDENS, Cardross, Dumbarton
Both gardens have been created within the last 15 years.
Kirkton Cottage (Mr & Mrs T C Duggan)
A garden of just less than one acre with mixed borders, shrubs, trees, herbs, vegetables, burn and ponds.
High Auchensail (Mr & Mrs M Wilson)
A wild woodland rhododendron and azalea garden with superb views over the Clyde. Plant stall at Kirkton Cottage. Cream teas at High Auchensail. Half mile and one mile respectively up Darleith Road at west end of Cardross village. No dogs please. Not suitable for wheelchairs.
Admission £2.00 includes both gardens   Children free
SUNDAY 7th JUNE 2 – 5pm
25% to R N L I   15% to Christian Aid

GEILSTON HOUSE, Cardross &

(The National Trust for Scotland)
This delightful property is representative of the small country houses and estates which pattern the banks of the Clyde and were developed as a result of the fortunes made in the City of Glasgow from tobacco and industrial development. The House (not open to the public) dates from the 15th century. The garden is charmingly simple, but with many attractive features including a walled garden and wooded glen. Plant stall on 30th May. Sorry no dogs. Cars free. Tea and shortbread. Cardross 1 mile. Route A814.
Admission £2.00 Children under 12 free
SATURDAY 30th MAY 2 - 5.30 pm
SUNDAY 19th JULY 2 - 5.30pm
40% to The Gardens Fund of The National Trust for Scotland

GLENARN, Rhu

(Michael & Sue Thornley and family)
Sheltered woodland garden overlooking the Gareloch, famous for its collection of rare and tender rhododendrons, together with fine magnolias and other ericaceous trees and shrubs. Beneath are snowdrops, crocus, daffodils, erithroniums and primulas in abundance. Improvements are underway in several areas. The pond is currently being reconstructed after vandalsism by a family of mallard ducks. Collection box at gate; dogs on leads please and cars to be left at gate unless passengers are infirm. On A814, two miles north of Helensburgh.
Minimum donation £1.50 Children and concessions £1.00
DAILY 21st MARCH to 21st SEPTEMBER sunrise – sunset
Special Opening SUNDAY 3rd MAY 2 – 5.30pm Home made teas and plant stall.
Admission £2.00 Children £1.00
40% the Dying Rooms Trust

THE HILL HOUSE, Helensburgh & (garden only)

(The National Trust for Scotland)
SCOTLAND'S GARDENS SCHEME PLANT SALE in garden. The Hill House overlooking the estuary of the River Clyde, is considered the finest example of the domestic architecture of Charles Rennie Mackintosh. The gardens are being restored to Walter W Blackie's design with features reflecting the work of Mackintosh.
Admission to Plant Sale free. Donations to SGS welcome
House open separately 1.30 - 5pm. Admission may be restricted.
SUNDAY 6th SEPTEMBER 11 am - 5 pm
40% to The Gardens Fund of the National Trust for Scotland
For other opening details see page 133

THE LINN GARDEN, Cove

(Mr James Taggart)
Extensive collections of trees, shrubs, bamboos and water plants surrounding a classical Victorian villa with fine views over the Firth of Clyde. Teas. Dogs on leads welcome. Entrance 1,100 yards north of Cove village on Shore Road, B833. No parking on Avenue; please park on shore side of main road.
Admission £3.00   OAPs £2.00 Students & teenagers £1.50 Children under 12 free
SUNDAY 17th MAY 2 – 6pm
40% to Shelter (Scotland)

ROSS PRIORY, Gartocharn ♿
(University of Strathclyde)
1812 Gothic addition by James Gillespie Graham to house of 1693 overlooking Loch
Lomond. Rhododendrons, azaleas, selected shrubs and trees. Walled garden with
glasshouses, alpine beds, pergola, ornamental plantings. Family burial ground. Nature
and garden trails. Putting Green. Baking and plant stalls. Tea in house. House not open
to view. Cars free. Gartocharn 1½ miles off A811. Bus: Balloch to Gartocharn leaves
Balloch at 1 pm and 3 pm.
Admission £1.50 Children free
SUNDAY 31st MAY 2 - 6 pm
20% to Enable 20% to Scottish Down's Syndrome Association

SHANDON GARDENS, Helensburgh
Ardchapel   (Mr & Mrs J S Lang)
Chapelburn   (Mr & Mrs W A Burnet)
Ardchapel Lodge   (Mr & Mrs C E Hudson)
Interesting combination of gardens overlooking the Gareloch, about six acres in all.
Rhododendrons, azaleas and other shrubs and trees. Wooded area with burn, bank of
bluebells. Well planned small cottage garden. Cup of tea and shortbread. Plant stall.
Baking stall and other attractions. Sorry no dogs. 3¾ miles north west of Helensburgh on
A814. Parking on service road below houses.
Admission £2.00 includes all gardens Children under 12 free OAPs £1.50
SUNDAY 24th MAY 2 5.30pm
40% to Sight Savers (Royal Commonwealth Society for the Blind)

EAST LOTHIAN

District Organiser:	**Lady Malcolm,** Whiteholm, Gullane EH31 2BD
Area Organisers:	**Mrs J Campbell Reid,** Kirklands, Gullane EH31 2AL
	Lady Fraser, Shepherd House, Inveresk, Musselburgh EH21 7TH
	Mrs C Gwyn, The Walled Garden, Tyninghame, Dunbar EH42 1XW
	Mrs M Ward, Stobshiel House, Humbie EH36 5PA
Hon Treasurer:	**Mr R McGee,** Royal Bank of Scotland, 32 Court Street, Haddington EH41 3NS

DATES OF OPENING

Winton House, Pencaitland	Sunday 18 April	2 – 6pm
Elvingston House, by Gladsmuir	Sunday 26 April	2 – 6pm
Tyninghame, Dunbar	Sunday 10 May	2 – 6pm

Inveresk: two gardens	Thursday 14 May	2 – 5pm
Stenton Village	Sunday 24 May	2 – 6pm
Dirleton Village	Sat&Sun 6/7 June	2 – 6pm
Bowerhouse, Spott, Dunbar	Sunday 14 June	2 – 6pm
Stevenson House, nr Haddington	Sunday 21 June	1 – 5pm
Inveresk: five gardens	Sat & Sun 27/28 June	2 - 5.30pm
Greywalls Hotel, Gullane	Monday 29 June	2 – 5pm
Forbes Lodge, Gifford	Sunday 5 July	2 – 6pm
Gifford Village	Sunday 5 July	2 – 6pm
Greywalls Hotel, Gullane	Monday 6 July	2 – 5pm
Luffness, Aberlady	Sunday 12 July	2 – 6pm
Tyninghame Village	Sunday 19 July	1.30–5.30pm
East Linton Gardens	Sunday 26 July	
Letham Mains, Haddington	Sunday 2 August	2 – 5pm
Pilmuir House, Haddington	Sunday 9 August	2 – 5pm
SGS Plant Sale, Oxenfoord Mains, Dalkeith	Sat&Sun 10/11 October	10.30am–3pm

BOWERHOUSE, Spott, Dunbar &

(Ian & Moira Marrian)
Bowerhouse is set in 26 acres of garden, orchard and woodland walks. There is an 18th century walled garden which is filled with a wide variety of flowers and shrubs, fruit and vegetables. Within the grounds, you can also find a doocot, wells, a pets graveyard and farmyard animals. Wildlife is attracted by thoughtful planting. The plant stall is being produced by the NCCPG Plant Heritage Lothians Group and will have many plants not easily available. Home made teas. Route: turn south at the Dunbar A1 bypass sign for Broomhouse and follow signs for half a mile.
Admission £2.00 Children and NCCPG members £1.00 Family ticket £5.00
SUNDAY 14th JUNE 2 – 6pm
40% to Save the Children Fund

DIRLETON VILLAGE &
Small gardens in beautiful village of
outstanding architectural interest. Historic
kirk and castle. Teas. Plant stall.
Admission £2.50 includes all gardens.
SATURDAY & SUNDAY
6th & 7th JUNE 2 - 6pm
40% to Dirleton Kirk

EAST LINTON GARDENS
Several gardens will be opening in this
attractive village – details will be published
closer to the opening day and posters
displayed locally.
SUNDAY 26th JULY
Charity to be advised

61

ELVINGSTON HOUSE, by Gladsmuir   ♿
(Dr David & Mrs Janice Simpson)
18th century garden of Jacobean-baronial mansion. A Caithness stone fountain on the
south lawn has been added recently and is surrounded by, in season, daffodils, 5,000
tulips and 1,000 roses. "Tetyana's Walk" is planted with roses, rhododendrons and
spring bulbs; there is also a Laburnum and Fuschia Walk. 18th century cylindrical
doocot with over 700 nesting boxes of ashlar stone. Teas. Dogs on lead please.
Route: 1 mile east of Gladsmuir, off A199 (old A1).
Admission £1.50 Children 50p Family Ticket £3.50
SUNDAY 26th APRIL 2 - 6pm
40% to Congenital Heart Disease Fund, Royal Hospital for Sick Children

FORBES LODGE, Gifford
(Lady Maryoth Hay)
Water garden. Old fashioned shrub roses. Burn. Stalls. Rare plants. Tea.
JOINT OPENING WITH GIFFORD VILLAGE GARDENS
Admission £1.00
SUNDAY 5th JULY 2 – 6 pm
40% to Children's League of Pity

GIFFORD VILLAGE GARDENS   ♿ (some)
Gifford is an attractive conservation village. Various gardens, small and large, in and
around the village will be open. Teas. Plant stall. Tickets and maps available from
several village and garden locations. Route: Follow B6369 from Haddington or B6355
from Tranent/Pencaitland.
JOINT OPENING WITH FORBES LODGE
Admission £2.50 includes all open gardens Children 20p
SUNDAY 5th JULY 2 – 6pm
40% to Children's League of Pity

GREYWALLS HOTEL, Gullane
(Mr & Mrs Giles Weaver)
Six acres of formal garden attributed to Gertrude Jekyll complements the Edwardian
house built by Sir Edwin Lutyens in 1901. Rose garden, herbaceous, shrub and annual
borders.
Admission £2.50 Accompanied children free
MONDAYS 29th JUNE & 6th JULY 2 - 5pm
40% to Leonard Cheshire Foundation in Scotland

INVERESK, near Musselburgh (two gardens)
Catherine Lodge (Mr Philip Mackenzie Ross)
A large well maintained garden with drifts of bulbs in spring. Magnificent herbaceous
and rose borders. Large traditional vegetable garden and greenhouses.
Shepherd House (Sir Charles & Lady Fraser)
A well planned one acre plantsman's garden with many unusual features, formal rill and
ponds, potager and parterre, alpine walk. Large collection of tulips.
No teas or stalls. Shepherd House also open by appointment : 0131 665 2570.
Admission £2.00 (includes both gardens). Accompanied children free
THURSDAY 14th MAY 2 - 5pm
40% to the Princess Royal Trust for Carers

INVERESK, near Musselburgh (five gardens)

Catherine Lodge	Mr Philip Mackenzie Ross
Eskhill House	Robin & Lindsay Burley (Sunday only)
Inveresk Lodge	The National Trust for Scotland
Oak Lodge	Mr & Mrs Michael Kennedy
Shepherd House	Sir Charles & Lady Fraser

Inveresk is a unique and unspoiled village on the southern fringes of Musselburgh.
There have been settlements here since Roman times. The present houses mostly date
from the late 17th and early 18th century. All have well laid out gardens enclosed by
high stone walls. Each garden has its own individual character – some formal, some less
so, some old, some new. They all contain a wide range of shrubs, trees and many
interesting and unusual plants. Plant stall. Teas on Sunday only.
Admission £3.50 OAPs £3.00 (includes all gardens). Accompanied children under 12 free.
SATURDAY & SUNDAY 27th & 28th JUNE 2 – 5.30pm
40% to the Princess Royal Trust for Carers

LETHAM MAINS, by Haddington
(Mr & Mrs Richard Edward)
New garden of approximately half an acre started in 1993 and developed from an
agricultural holding. Several water features including ornamental bridge, working water
wheel and waterfalls. Variety of new tree plantings, herbaceous beds, alpines, heathers
and conifers. Rockeries built from naturally weathered stone are also a main feature.
Teas. Located one mile from Haddington on A6093. No dogs please.
Admission £2.00 Children free
SUNDAY 2nd AUGUST 2 – 5pm
40% to Cancer Research

LUFFNESS, Aberlady ᪥ (weather permitting)
(Luffness Limited)
16th century castle with earlier foundations. Fruit garden built by Napoleonic prisoners-
of-war. Tea in house. Plant stall. Donations please.
SUNDAY 12th JULY 2 - 6 pm
40% to Scottish Society for the Prevention of Cruelty to Animals

---

PILMUIR HOUSE, Haddington ᪥
(Sir Henry Wade's Pilmuir Trust)
Four acre walled garden with 17th century doocot and interesting collection of mature
trees and shrubs. Formal garden area with bee boles currently under restoration with
box edged borders, roses and herbaceous plants. Kitchen garden being re-established as
part of long term programme of work begun last year. Further two acres of woodland
areas. Teas. Plant stall. Route: B6355 from Pencaitland to East Saltoun. First left at East
Saltoun, after one mile fork right, first turning on left.
Admission £2.00 Children 75p Family ticket £5.00
SUNDAY 9th AUGUST 2 – 5pm
40% to Sir Henry Wade's Pilmuir Trust

STENTON VILLAGE GARDENS ♿ (some)
Stenton is a conservation village considered to be the best preserved in East Lothian. Several varied and interesting gardens in and around the village will be open. Teas and maps available in the Village Hall. A festival of flowers in Stenton Parish Church. Follow signs from A1 East Linton/Dunbar.
Admission £2.00 to include all open gardens. Children £1.00 Family ticket £5.00
SUNDAY 24th MAY 2 – 6pm
40% to British Red Cross Society, East Lothian branch

STEVENSON HOUSE, near Haddington ♿
(Mrs J C H Dunlop)
House garden includes wide lawns surrounded by large flowerbeds containing a mixture of herbaceous plants and shrubs, a rose garden, spring border and rock edge. Woods and dell containing many fine trees. Formal walled garden, many unusual plantings. Plant stall. Riverside walk. Stevenson House marked on A1 between Haddington & East Linton. Historic House signs on A1 and on road from Haddington.
Admission to grounds, including parking £2.50 Children under 12 free
SUNDAY 21st JUNE 1 – 5 pm
20% to Malcolm Sargent Cancer Fund for Children 20% to Save the Children Fund

---

TYNINGHAME, Dunbar ♿
(Tyninghame Gardens Ltd)
Splendid 17th century pink sandstone Scottish baronial house, remodelled in 1829 by William Burn, rises out of a sea of plants. Herbaceous border, formal rose garden, Lady Haddington's secret garden with old fashioned roses, formal walled garden with sculpture and yew hedges. The 'wilderness' spring garden with magnificent rhododendrons, azaleas, flowering trees and bulbs. Grounds include one mile beech avenue to sea, famous 'apple walk', Romanesque ruin of St Baldred's Church, views across parkland to Tyne estuary and Lammermuir Hills. Tyninghame 1 mile.
Admission £2.00 Children free
SUNDAY 10th MAY 2 – 6 pm
40% to East Linton Support Group for St Columba's and Marie Curie Hospice

---

 # TYNINGHAME VILLAGE GARDENS ♿ (some)
A variety of gardens in historic estate village. Plant stall. Teas in Village Hall. Route: A198 off the A1.
Admission £1.50 includes all open gardens Children 50p
SUNDAY 19th JULY 1.30 – 5.30pm
40% to Action Aid

WINTON HOUSE, Pencaitland
(Winton Trust)
17th century Renaissance house. Decorative stone chimneys and dormers. William Wallace, master mason. Early 19th century castellated entrance. Beautiful plaster ceilings and stone carving, fine pictures and furniture. Masses of daffodils. Fine trees, terraced gardens. House conducted tour: £3.50, OAPs £3, children under 14 £2. Tea and biscuits in house. Paintings, crafts and home baking. Plant nursery and pottery in grounds. From Pencaitland, lodge & wrought-iron gates two-thirds mile on A6093, or, on B6355, archway and wrought-iron gates 1 mile from New Winton village, drive ½ mile.
Admission £2.00 Children £1.00 Family ticket £5.00
SATURDAY 18th APRIL 2 – 6 pm
40% to Royal Commonwealth Society for the Blind (Sight Savers)

ARDKINGLAS, Argyll (Mr S J Noble)   *Sunday 14th June 11am–5pm*
Photograph by Ray Whitfield, winner of 1997 Photographic Competition

50 RANKIN STREET, GREENOCK, Renfrew & Inverclyde
(Mr & Mrs Fred Ball) *Sunday 19th July 1.30 –5.30pm*
Photograph by Fred Ball

CRAIL: Small Gardens in the Burgh, Fife
(The Gardeners of Crail) *Saturday & Sunday 25th & 26th July 2 – 5.30pm*
Photograph by Mrs A B Cran

DOWHILL, Cleish, Perth & Kinross
(Mr & Mrs C Maitland Dougall)   *Sunday 7th June 2 – 5pm*
Photograph by Mrs C Maitland Dougall

ARDCHAPEL, SHANDON GARDENS, Dunbartonshire West
(Mr & Mrs J S Lang) *Sunday 24th May 2–5.30pm*
Photograph by Mrs J S Lang

NETHERBYRES, Eyemouth, Berwickshire
(Col S J Furness & GRBS) *Sunday 19th April & Sunday 19th July 2 – 6pm*
Photograph by Col S J Furness

BLAIRQUHAN, Straiton, Maybole, Ayrshire
(Mr James Hunter Blair)   *Sunday 16th August 1.30 – 4.30pm*
Photograph by Adrian Thomas

BARGANY, Girvan, Ayrshire
(N J F Dalrymple Hamilton)   *1st March – 31st October 10am–7pm or dusk*
Photograph by Brian Chapple

SGS PLANT SALE
A Bring and Buy Plant Sale will be held under cover at Oxenfoord Mains, Dalkeith on
SATURDAY 10th OCTOBER 1 – 4pm
SUNDAY 11th OCTOBER 10.30am – 3pm.
Route: 4 miles south of Dalkeith on A68, turn left for one mile on A6093.
Admission free.

EDINBURGH & WEST LOTHIAN

Joint District Organisers:	**Mrs J C Monteith,** 7 West Stanhope Place, Edinburgh EH12 5HQ
	Mrs Charles Welwood, Kirknewton House, Kirknewton, West Lothian EH27 8DA
Joint Hon. Treasurers:	**Mrs J C Monteith and Mrs Charles Welwood**

DATES OF OPENING

13 Belford Place, Edinburgh .... 1 April to 31 July by appointment
Newliston, Kirkliston .... Wednesdays to Sundays inclusive
1 May – 4 June   2 – 6pm

Dalmeny Park, South Queensferry .... Date to be announced
Dean Gardens & Ann Street, Edinburgh .... Sunday 5 April   2 – 6pm
Foxhall, Kirkliston .... Sunday 19 April   2 – 5.30pm
Hethersett, Balerno .... Sunday 26 April   2 – 5.30pm
Redhall Walled Garden, Edinburgh .... Saturday 2 May   10am-3pm
Hermiston House, Currie .... Sunday 3 May   2 – 5pm
Dr Neil's Garden, Duddingston .... Sat & Sun 9/10 May   2 – 5pm
Redhall Walled Garden, Edinburgh .... Saturday 30 May   10am-3pm
Kirknewton House, Kirknewton .... Sat & Sun 13/14 June   2-6pm
Arthur Lodge, Dalkeith Road, Edinburgh .... Sunday 21 June   2 – 5pm
Malleny Garden, Balerno .... Wednesday 24 June   2 – 5pm
Dr Neil's Garden, Duddingston .... Sat & Sun 8/9 August   2 – 5pm
Redhall Walled Garden, Edinburgh .... Saturday 15 August   10am-3pm
Suntrap Horticultural Centre, Edinburgh .... Sunday 23 August   2 – 5pm
SGS Plant Sale, Kirknewton House .... Sat&Sun 26/27 September 11.30am–4pm

13 BELFORD PLACE, Edinburgh

(Mr & Mrs G Severn)

1½ acre hillside garden in centre of town. Unusual plants, shrubs and ground cover, pond. Entrance beyond Edinburgh Sports Club.

Admission £2.00

1st APRIL to 31st JULY by appointment. Tel: (0131) 332 2104

40% to Home Link

ARTHUR LODGE, 60 Dalkeith Road, Edinburgh &

(Mr S R Friden)

Formal herbaceous garden. Sunken Italian garden and White garden. Plant stall. Entrance to garden in Blacket Place, opposite the Commonwealth Pool.

Admission £1.50 Children £1.00

SUNDAY 21st JUNE 2 - 5pm

40% to Cockburn Association (Pinkerton Fund)

DALMENY PARK, South Queensferry

(The Earl & Countess of Rosebery)

Acres of snowdrops on Mons Hill. Cars free. Teas will be available in the Courtyard Tearoom, Dalmeny House. Route: South Queensferry, off A90 road to B924. Pedestrians and cars enter by Leuchold Gate and exit by Chapel Gate.

Admission £2.00 Children under 14 free

DATE TO BE ANNOUNCED

40% to St Columba's Hospice

DEAN GARDENS & ANN STREET, Edinburgh

DEAN GARDENS (Dean Gardens Committee of Management)

Privately owned town gardens on north bank of the Water of Leith. 13½ acres of spring bulbs, daffodils, trees and shrubs and other interesting features. Entrance at Ann Street or Eton Terrace.

ANN STREET GARDENS

Ann Street is one of the few Georgian streets where the houses on both sides boast their own front gardens. They are particularly pretty in spring and early summer with flowering trees, shrubs and bulbs.

Admission to both gardens £1.00 Children 50p

SUNDAY 5th APRIL 2 - 6 pm

40% to the Gardens Fund of the National Trust for Scotland

DR NEIL'S GARDEN, Duddingston Village

(Drs Andrew & Nancy Neil)

Landscaped garden on the lower slopes of Arthur's Seat using conifers, heathers and alpines. Teas in Kirk Hall. Plant stalls. Car park on Duddingston Road West.

Admission £1.50 Children free

SATURDAY & SUNDAY 9th & 10th MAY 2 - 5 pm

SATURDAY & SUNDAY 8th & 9th AUGUST 2 - 5 pm

All takings to Scotland's Gardens Scheme

FOXHALL, Kirkliston
(Mr & Mrs James Gammell)
Daffodils and woodland walk. Plant stall. Cake stall. Turn east at lights in centre of
Kirkliston, half mile on right, sign at road end, Conifox Nursery.
Admission £2.00 Children under 14 free OAPs £1.00
SUNDAY 19th APRIL 2 - 5.30 pm
40% to St Columba's Hospice

 # HERMISTON HOUSE, Currie &
(Heriot-Watt University)
Formal garden and woodland walk. Walled kitchen garden/nursery. Overlooks the
Union Canal. No dogs please. Teas, weather permitting. Route: A71 from Edinburgh,
first right after Calder roundabout, first left to Hermiston.
Admission £2.00 Children under 12 free
SUNDAY 3rd MAY 2 – 5pm
40% to Shelter Scotland

HETHERSETT, Balerno
(Professor & Mrs I G Stewart)
Informal, woodland garden with daffodils, primulas and rhododendrons. No dogs
please. Plant stall. Teas. In Balerno, off Lanark Road West (A70). Cars enter by Larch
Grove Lodge opposite Malleny House, NTS.
Admission £2.00 Children 50p
SUNDAY 26th APRIL 2 – 5.30pm
40% to Friends of the Royal Botanic Garden Edinburgh

KIRKNEWTON HOUSE, Kirknewton &
(Mr & Mrs Charles Welwood)
Extensive woodland garden. Rhododendrons, azaleas and shrubs. Teas, weather
permitting. No dogs please. Route: Either A71 or A70 on to B7031.
Admission £2.00 Children under 14 free
SATURDAY & SUNDAY 13th & 14th JUNE 2 - 6pm
40% to St Columba's Hospice

KIRKNEWTON HOUSE, Kirknewton &
SGS Bring & Buy PLANT SALE
SATURDAY & SUNDAY 26th & 27th SEPTEMBER 11.30am – 4pm
40% to Childrens Hospice Association Scotland

MALLENY GARDEN, Balerno &
(The National Trust for Scotland)
A three acre walled garden with 17th century clipped yew trees, lawns and borders.
Wide and varied selection of herbaceous plants and shrubs. Shrub roses including
NCCPG. 19th century rose collection. Ornamental vegetable and herb garden.
Greenhouse display. Scottish National Bonsai Collection. Plant stall. Tea and biscuits.
In Balerno, off Lanark Road West (A70) 7m from Edinburgh city centre. Buses: Lothian
43, Eastern Scottish, 66 & 44.
Admission £1.00 Children & OAPs 50p
WEDNESDAY 24th JUNE 2 - 5 pm
40% to The Gardens Fund of The National Trust for Scotland
For other opening details see page 131

NEWLISTON, Kirkliston ♿
(Mr & Mrs R C Maclachlan)
18th century designed landscape. Rhododendrons and azaleas. The house, which was designed by Robert Adam, is open and a collection of costumes will be on display. Teas. On Sundays tea is in the Edinburgh Cookery School which operates in the William Adam Coach House. Also on Sundays there is a ride-on steam model railway from 2 - 5 pm. 4 miles from Forth Road Bridge, entrance off B800.
Admission: House & Garden £1.00
Children & OAPs 50p
WEDNESDAYS - SUNDAYS inclusive each week from1st MAY to 4th JUNE 2 - 6pm
40% to Children's Hospice Association Scotland

REDHALL WALLED GARDEN,
97 Lanark Road, Edinburgh ♿
(Scottish Association for Mental Health)
A traditional walled garden built in the 18th century. Now a listed garden it is run on organic principles as a mental health project. Teas. Barbeque. Large selection of annuals, shrubs and herbaceous plants.
Admission £1.00 Concessions free
SATURDAYS 2nd & 30th MAY
and 15th AUGUST 10am - 3pm
40% to Scottish Association for Mental Health

SUNTRAP HORTICULTURAL & GARDENING CENTRE 43 Gogarbank, Edinburgh
(Oatridge Agricultural College, organised by Friends of Suntrap) ♿
A horticultural out-centre of Oatridge Agricultural College. Compact garden of 1.7 hectares (3 acres), includes rock and water features, sunken garden, raised beds, woodland plantings & greenhouses. Facilities for professional and amateur instruction, horticultural advice and a place to visit. Home baking. Plant sales. Gardening advice. Parking for disabled drivers inside main gate, other car parking opposite. Signposted 0.5m west of Gogar roundabout, off A8 and 0.25m west of Calder Junction (City bypass) off A71. Bus route: Lothian Transit 37. Open daily throughout the year 9am –4.30 pm. Friends of Suntrap in garden at weekends, April to September 2.30 – 4.30pm.
Admission £1.00 Children & OAPs 50p
SUNDAY 23rd AUGUST 2 - 5pm
40% to The National Trust for Scotland (Harmony House Garden, Melrose)

ETTRICK & LAUDERDALE

District Organiser: **Mrs Gavin Younger,** Chapel-on-Leader, Earlston TD4 6AW

DATES OF OPENING

Bemersyde, Melrose	Sunday 26 April	2 – 6pm
Chapel-on-Leader, Earlston	Sunday 5 July	2 – 6pm
Abbotsford, Melrose	Sunday 2 August	2 – 5.30pm

ABBOTSFORD, Melrose ♿ (partly)
(Mrs P Maxwell-Scott, OBE)
House and garden built and laid out by Sir
Walter Scott, who built the house 1812-1832
when he died. Herbaceous and annual borders.
Teashop in grounds. Jedburgh Branch Royal
British Legion Pipe Band. Admission to house
and garden: £3.50, children £1.80. Bus party -
adults £2.50, children £1.30. Melrose 2 miles,
Galashiels 1½ miles.
Admission to garden only: £2.00
SUNDAY 2nd AUGUST   2 - 5.30 pm
40% to Marie Curie Cancer Care
(Borders branch)

BEMERSYDE, Melrose ♿
(The Earl Haig)
16th century peel tower reconstructed in the
17th century with added mansion house.
Garden laid out by Field Marshal Earl Haig.
Views of Eildon Hills. Woodland walks.
Admission to garden only. St Boswells via
Clintmains or Melrose via Leaderfoot Bridge.
Admission £1.65 Children under 10 free
SUNDAY 26th APRIL 2 - 6 pm
40% to Lady Haig's Poppy Factory

CHAPEL-ON-LEADER, Earlston
♿ (with help)
(Mr & Mrs Gavin Younger)
Large country garden with lovely views of
park and river. Inspired by Sissinghurst and
Jekyll, planting is informal with interesting
foliage as well as flowers. Divided into different areas there is a white garden, rose
avenue, azalea border, mixed borders with old fashioned roses, clematis and rose covered
pergolas, paved swimming pool area, recently restored water and bog garden, woodland
and rhododendron walks and a large walled kitchen garden. Home made teas. Plant
stall. Turn off A68 at sign 2m north of Earlston, 4m south of Lauder.
Admission £2.00 Children free
SUNDAY 5th JULY 2 - 6pm
40% to Save the Children Fund

FIFE

District Organiser: **Mrs David L Skinner**, Lathrisk House, Freuchie KY15 7HX

Area Organisers: **Mrs J Auchinleck,** 2 Castle Street, Crail KY10 3SQ
Mrs James Barr, Burnbank, Drumhead, Saline KY12 9LL
Mrs A B Cran, Karbet, Freuchie KY15 7EY
Mrs Ian Crombie, West Hall, Cupar KY15 4NA
Mrs Christine Gordon, The Tannery, Kilconquhar,
   Leven KY9 1LQ
Mrs Roderick F Jones, Nether Kinneddar, Saline KY12 9LJ
Lady Spencer Nairn, Barham, Bow of Fife KY15 5RG
Mrs N Stewart-Meiklejohn, 6 Howard Place,
   St Andrews KY16 9HL

Hon. Treasurer: **Mrs C Erskine,** Cambo House, Kingsbarns KY16 8QD

DATES OF OPENING

Cambo House, Kingsbarns	Daily all year 10am – 5pm	
Cambo House, Kingsbarns	Sunday 22 Feb (provisionally)	2 – 5pm
The Murrel, Aberdour	Sat & Sun 25/26 April	10am–5pm
Barham, Bow of Fife	Sunday 3 May	12 – 4pm
Birkhill, Cupar	Sunday 10 May	12.30–4pm
Cambo House, Kingsbarns	Sunday 17 May	2 – 5pm
Spring Plant Sale at Karbet, Freuchie	Sunday 7 June	11am–4pm
Culross Palace Garden	Sunday 14 June	11am–5pm
Parleyhill, Culross	Sunday 14 June	11am–5pm
Balcaskie, Pittenweem	Sunday 21 June	2 – 5pm
Micklegarth, Aberdour	Sunday 21 June	2 – 5pm
3 Gardens near Newburgh	Sunday 28 June	11am–4pm
Hidden gardens of St Andrews	Sunday 28 June	11am–6pm
St Andrews Botanic Garden	Sunday 28 June	10am–6pm
Cambo House, Kingsbarns	Sunday 5 July	2 – 6pm
Kellie Castle, Pittenweem	Sunday 5 July	11am–5pm
Blebocraigs Village Gardens	Sunday 12 July	1.30–5.30pm
Lathrisk House & Old Lathrisk, Freuchie	Sunday 12 July	2–5.30pm
Hidden gardens of Strathkinness	Sat & Sun 18/19 July	2 – 5pm
Crail Gardens	Sat & Sun 25/26 July	2–5.30pm
Naughton, by Wormit	Sunday 26 July	11am–5pm
Peacehaven, Lundin Links	Saturday 1 August	2 – 5pm
Ladies Lake, St Andrews	Sunday 9 August(provisionally)	2 – 5pm
Falkland Palace Garden	Sunday 9 August	1.30–5pm
Hill of Tarvit, Cupar	Sunday 16 August	12.30–5pm
SGS Plant Sale, Hill of Tarvit, by Cupar	Saturday 3 October	10.30am–4pm
	Sunday 4 October	1–4pm

BALCASKIE, Pittenweem ♿ (top terrace only)
(Sir Ralph Anstruther of that Ilk Bt.)
There has been a house, originally fortified, at Balcaskie since the 13th century and a charter granted to Ivor Cook by King Alexander III in 1223 exists. In 1665 Sir William Bruce altered the tower house, laid out the terraces and made what he called " the first mansion house in Scotland". He lived there before building, and moving to, Kinross house. The Anstruther family acquired the property in 1698. Teas. Stalls. East Neuk Pipe Band. Route: A917, 2 miles from Anstruther. Enter by west Lodge gate.
Admission £2.00 Children free
SUNDAY 21st JUNE 2 – 5 pm
40% to SSAFA Forces Help

BARHAM, Bow of Fife ♿
(Sir Robert & Lady Spencer Nairn)
A garden full of character and friends. A small woodland garden in the making with rhododendrons, shrubs, spring bulbs and ferns. Also a garden with herbaceous borders and island beds with shrubs and spring bulbs and a vegetable garden. Plant stall. Hot soup and rolls. Route: A91, 4 miles west of Cupar. No dogs please.
Admission £2.00 Children under 12 free
SUNDAY 3rd MAY 12 - 4pm
40% to Pain Association Scotland

BIRKHILL, Cupar ♿
(The Earl & Countess of Dundee)
Traditional walled garden. Spring woodland garden which has been restored and extended with rare magnolias and rhododendrons. Woodland, cliff and beach walks.
Cottage Garden (Mr & Mrs Lumsden)
An exceptional alpine garden and good plant stall.
Soup and rolls. Produce stall. Pony rides.
Admission to include both gardens: £2.50
SUNDAY 10th MAY 12.30 – 4 pm
40% to Luthrie School

 # BLEBOCRAIGS VILLAGE GARDENS ♿ (some, partially)
Rare opening of gardens in this former quarry village. The gardens, most with attractive rural views, are of many different styles and approaches, from new gardens to organic, florist's garden to "hidden" gardens. Teas. Plant stall. No dogs please. Route: 7 miles from St Andrews on B939 between Pitscottie and Strathkinness. Free parking on grass opposite Village Hall.
Admission £2.50 includes all open gardens Accompanied children free
SUNDAY 12th JULY 1.30 – 5.30 pm
40% to Blebocraigs Village Hall

CAMBO HOUSE, Kingsbarns &

(Mr & Mrs T P N Erskine)

An enchanting unusual Victorian walled garden designed around the Cambo burn which runs through the garden and is spanned by ornamental bridges and a greenhouse. The garden supplies the superb Victorian mansion house (not open) with flowers, fruit and vegetables. An ornamental potager was started in 1997. Woodland walks along the burn leading to the beach. The season starts with acres of snowdrops and snowflakes. Massed daffodils and spring bulbs follow. A lilac walk, over 250 named roses and herbaceous borders in summer. September borders and colchicum meadow give autumn interest. Cars free. Dogs on lead please. Route: A917.

Admission £2.00 Children free

SNOWDROP DAY: Provisionally SUNDAY 22nd FEBRUARY 2 - 5pm Plant stall. Teas.
40% to Romania Link
SPRING OPENING: SUNDAY 17th MAY 2 - 5 pm Plant Stall. Teas.
40% to British Diabetic Association
ROSE OPENING: SUNDAY 5th JULY 2 - 6pm Refreshments
40% to Rose 2000 Appeal, Royal National Rose Society
OPEN ALL YEAR ROUND 10 am - 5 pm

CRAIL: SMALL GARDENS IN THE BURGH

(The Gardeners of Crail)

A number of small gardens in varied styles: cottage, historic, plantsman's, bedding. Exhibition of paintings at Lobster Cottage, Shoregate. Approach Crail from either St Andrews or Anstruther, A917. Park in the Marketgate. Tickets and map available only from Mrs Auchinleck, 2 Castle Street, Crail.

Admission £2.50 Acccompanied Children free OAPs £1.50
SATURDAY & SUNDAY 25th and 26th JULY 2 - 5.30 pm
20% to Children's Hospice Association Scotland 20% to Crail Preservation Society

---

CULROSS PALACE GARDEN, Culross

(The National Trust for Scotland)

Built between 1597 and 1611, the house was not a Royal Palace, but the home of Sir George Bruce, a rich merchant. It features painted ceilings and has recently been restored and furnished. A model 17th century garden was created at the same time as the house restoration, and reflects what a successful merchant of the period might have grown to support his household - vegetables, culinary and medicinal herbs, soft fruit and flowering meads. Terraced and on a steep slope, it is laid out mainly in raised beds. Sections are partitioned by willow hurdle fences, and the path surface is made up of crushed shells.

Admission to Palace, garden, Town House & Study £4.20, concessions £2.80 Family £11.20

Admission to garden £1.00 Children & OAPs 50p
SUNDAY 14th JUNE 11am - 5pm
40% to The Gardens Fund of the National Trust for Scotland
For other opening details see page 126

FALKLAND PALACE GARDEN, Falkland &

(The National Trust for Scotland)
The Royal Palace of Falkland, set in the heart of a medieval village, was the country residence and hunting lodge of eight Stuart monarchs, including Mary, Queen of Scots. The palace gardens were restored by the late Keeper, Major Michael Crichton Stuart, to a design by Percy Cane. Tearooms nearby in village. Free car park. Route: A912.
Admission to Palace and garden £4.80, concessions £3.20 Family £12.80
Admission to Garden £2.40 Children £1.60
SUNDAY 9th AUGUST 1.30 - 5 pm
40% to The Gardens Fund of the National Trust for Scotland
For other opening details see page 126

HILL OF TARVIT, by Cupar

(The National Trust for Scotland)
Both house and garden were remodelled by Sir Robert Lorimer in 1906 and the result is a wonderful mix of formal gardens and parkland. Visitors can wander through the fragrant walled garden with its herbaceous borders, linger on the terraces catching glimpses of the glorious view through ornamental yes, or enjoy the heady rose scent in the sunken garden. Tea room. Plant stall.
Route A916. Admission to house and garden: £3.70, concesssions £2.50 Family £9.90
Admission to garden: £1.00 Children & OAPs 50p
SUNDAY 16th AUGUST 12.30 - 5 pm
40% to The Gardens Fund of The National Trust for Scotland
For other opening details see page 127

SCOTLAND'S GARDENS SCHEME PLANT SALE
at Hill of Tarvit, by Cupar

(The National Trust for Scotland)
Bring plants, buy plants. Large variety of shrubs and big clumps of herbaceous plants at bargain prices. Route: A916.
Saturday – Coffee & snack lunches.   Sunday – Teas.
SATURDAY 3rd OCTOBER 10.30am – 4pm   SUNDAY 4th OCTOBER 1 – 4pm
40% to East Fife Members Centre of The National Trust for Scotland

---

KELLIE CASTLE, Pittenweem &

(The National Trust for Scotland)
A delightful model of a late Victorian garden, with box-edged paths, rose arches and many herbaceous plants and roses of the period. The organic gardening methods used here make Kellie an inspiring garden to visit. Tearoom. Adventure playground. Good picnic area.
Admission to Garden £1.00 Children & OAPs 50p
SUNDAY 5th JULY 11 am - 5 pm
40% to The Gardens Fund of the National Trust for Scotland
For further opening details see page 129

FIFE

LADIES LAKE, The Scores, St Andrews ♿ (with help - some steps)
(Mr & Mrs Gordon T Senior)
The garden is small, no more than half an acre. It occupies a saucer-shaped curve on the
cliff adjacent to St Andrews Castle. In essence, the garden consists of two terraces, one of
which is cantilevered over the sea. About 6,000 bedding plants are crammed into half a
dozen beds. Teas. Plant stall. Route: from North Street, turn left into North Castle
Street, left in front of castle and house is 150 yards on right.
Admission £2.00 Accompanied children free
SUNDAY 9th AUGUST (provisionally) 2 – 5pm
40% to Hope Park Church, St Andrews

LATHRISK HOUSE & OLD LATHRISK, Freuchie ♿ (with help)
(Mr & Mrs David Skinner and Mr & Mrs David Wood)
These adjoining gardens boast a large variety of trees from abies to yews in a beautiful
setting with views over the Howe of Fife and East Lomond. The Georgian Lathrisk
House reveals new treasures in its ever changing herbaceous borders, raised bed and
container planting. Old Lathrisk, dating from the 17th century, has an informal
woodland garden incorporating, at one end, a potager containing a large variety of
insects, birds and mammals, and at the other end, a rustic fly-over to a short burnside
walk. Teas. Good plant stall. Traditional jazz. No dogs please. Off A914 on outskirts of
Freuchie or B936 Falkland/Newton of Falkland.
Admission £2.00 Children free
SUNDAY 12th JULY 2 – 5.30pm
40% to Falkland Parish Church

MICKLEGARTH, Aberdour
(Gordon & Kathleen Maxwell)
Small, informal garden with shrubbery, herbaceous and island beds and rock garden.
Plant & produce stall. In heart of historic seaside village. Route: A921. Train, bus or car
to Aberdour, park in car park at railway station; proceed west along High Street
approximately 200 metres.
Admission £1.50 Accompanied children free
SUNDAY 21st JUNE 2 - 5 pm
40% to Childrens Hospice Association Scotland

THE MURREL, Aberdour
(Mrs John E Milne)
BIG PLANT SALE: There are now surplus plants from the garden which will be potted
up for the sale.
This garden, which was planted in 1982 is now well established and filled with
interesting and unusual plants. There are water gardens and woodland walks, a rose
garden and a walled garden. Not suitable for wheelchairs. No dogs please. On B9157
Inverkeithing/Kirkcaldy road, opposite Croftgarry Farm.
Admission £1.00
SATURDAY and SUNDAY 25th & 26th APRIL 10am – 5pm
Donation to Scotland's Gardens Scheme

NAUGHTON, by Wormit
(Dr Britt Marie Crawford)
The garden is within the ruins of the 13th century Naughton Castle situated on an elevation behind the mansion house. The plantings, all made in the past four years, are of herbaceous perennials, many rare and unusual. Plants for sale are propagated from the garden. Surrounding the house are many mature specimen trees of interest. Teas. Plant stall. No dogs please. Off A914, two miles west of Wormit on the Balmerino road.
Admission £2.00 Accompanied children free
SUNDAY 26th JULY 11am – 5pm
40% to Gauldry Village Hall Fund

THREE GARDENS NEAR NEWBURGH ♿ (with help)
Three substantially sized gardens in the process of being created, within a diameter of one mile, best visited in the order in which they are described here.
Easter Dunbog (Major & Mrs C B Innes)
Charming 18th century former manse with walled garden and small orchard. The present owners set about restoring both house and garden in 1996. The garden is still very much in the making. Herbaceous and shrub borders. Roses.
Admission £1.00 Children under 16 free
Balmeadow (Mr & Mrs S Fontes)
A walled cottage garden plus an informal garden created from an acre paddock during the last five years, containing island shrub beds, an herbaceous border, many shrub roses and varieties of trees. No dogs please. Soup and rolls.
Admission £1.00 Children under 16 free
Aytounhill House (Mr & Mrs Neil Findlay)
A new garden created from a field, now in its 7th year. Several mixed borders with a wide variety of shrubs and herbaceous plants. Splendid situation. Walk round loch. Home made teas. Plant stall. No dogs please.
Admission £2.00 Children under 16 free
All the gardens are off the A913, 7 miles from Cupar and 7 miles from Newburgh.
Inclusive tickets at £4.00 can be bought at any of the gardens.
SUNDAY 28th JUNE 11am – 4pm
40% to Abdie & Dunbog Parish Church

PARLEYHILL GARDEN, Culross
(Mr & Mrs R J McDonald)
Overlooking the Forth and the historic village of Culross this delightful hidden garden is bordered by high stone walls and lies beside Culross Abbey and the adjacent Culross Abbey ruins. Pass around the house via the upper 'cool' garden (established in the early '60s) with its mature trees and a variety of shaded beds to discover the lower walled garden (dating from 1988) and its views. Here, take the chance to have a seat and enjoy the wide variety of plants and colourful display in the herbaceous borders full of old fashioned favourites like phlox, crocosmia, irises, asters etc. Plant stall selling a selection of plants from the garden. No dogs please. Free parking in village.
Admission £1.50 Accompanied children free
SUNDAY 14th JUNE 11am - 5pm with Culross Palace Garden
40% to Culross and Torryburn Church

PEACEHAVEN, Lundin Links   ♿

(Peter & Kim Nimmo)

A riot of summer colours, clever use of containers and a sunken garden created by the Beechgrove Garden Hit Squad. Home baked teas. Plant and cake stalls.

Lundin Links is on A915 between Leven and Upper Largo.

Admission £1.00 Children free

SATURDAY 1st AUGUST 2 – 5pm

40% to Childrens Hospice Association

THE HIDDEN GARDENS OF ST ANDREWS   ♿ (some)

About a dozen gardens in old St Andrews, most of them opening for the first time, ranging from the tiniest courtyard to traditional 'long riggs'. An opportunity to explore the closes and wynds of the medieval town. A number of gardens will provide teas and refreshment. Plant stall. Tickets and plans from the National Trust for Scotland shop and all open gardens.

Admission £3.00 includes all open gardens Children free

SUNDAY 28th JUNE 11am – 6pm

40% to The St Andrews Preservation Trust

ST ANDREWS BOTANIC GARDEN, Canongate, St Andrews ♿

(Fife Council)

Peat, rock and water gardens. Tree, shrub, bulb and herbaceous borders. Large range of plants under glass. Plant stall. Route: A915. Well signposted in St Andrews.

Admission £2.00 Accompanied children £1.00

SUNDAY 28th JUNE 10 am – 6 pm

40% to Friends of the Botanic Garden

THE HIDDEN GARDENS OF STRATHKINNESS   ♿

A variety of cottage gardens featuring herbaceous, roses, summer bedding and patio planters. Teas and plant stall in Village Hall where tickets and instructions will be issued. Well signposted from A91 Cupar/St Andrews and St Andrews/Cupar road via Pitscottie. NB Take care at both crossroad junctions at top and bottom of village.

Admission £2.50 includes all open gardens   Children free

SATURDAY & SUNDAY 18th & 19th JULY 2 – 5pm

40% Strathkinness Parish Church Hall Building Fund

SPRING PLANT SALE in Freuchie   ♿ (with help)

(Major & Mrs A B Cran)

A wide selection of plants both annual and perennial and of shrubs will be on sale at Karbet in the centre of Freuchie on the B936. Teas.

Admission £1.00 Children free

SUNDAY 7th JUNE 11am – 4pm

40% to SSAFA Forces Help

GLASGOW & DISTRICT

District Organiser:	**Mrs J Thomson,** Hexagon House, Bardowie Loch G62 6EY
Area Organisers:	**Mrs S Bell,** 9 Station Road, Bardowie G62 6ET
	Mrs C M T Donaldson, 2 Edgehill Road, Bearsden G61 3AD
	Mrs A Wardlaw, 92 Drymen Road, Bearsden G61 2SY
Hon. Treasurer:	**Mr M Smith,** Lanercost, 84 Busby Road, Carmunnock G76 9BJ

DATES OF OPENING

Bystone Mews, Clarkston .... May – August by appointment
Invermay, Cambuslang .... April – September by appointment
Six Fathoms, Eaglesham .... July and August by appointment

Greenbank House & Garden, Clarkston	Saturday 28 February	11am – 5pm
Greenbank House & Garden, Clarkston	Saturday 9 May	11am – 5pm
65 Montgomerie Street, Eaglesham	Sunday 7 June	2 – 5pm
44 Gordon Road, Netherlee	Sunday 14 June	2 – 5pm
Kittoch Mill, Carmunnock	Sunday 21 June	2 – 5pm
Torrance Demonstration Garden	Sunday 28 June	2 – 5pm
Kittoch Mill, Carmunnock	Sunday 5 July	2 – 5pm
Bystone Mews, Clarkston	Sunday 19 July	2 – 5pm
Six Fathoms, Eaglesham	Sunday 2 August	2 – 5pm
Whitemoss House, East Kilbride	Sunday 2 August	2 – 5pm
Glasgow Botanic Gardens	Sunday 16 August	12–4.30pm

44 GORDON ROAD, Netherlee
(Mr & Mrs James G Murray)
Mature town garden of approximately one acre on edge of woodland. Large trees, rhododendrons planted in the 1930s. Herbaceous border and beds with many unusual plants. Plant stall. No dogs please. B767 Clarkston Road past Linn Park gates. Turn at Williamwood Drive, then second turning left.
Admission £1.50 Children over 12 50p
SUNDAY 14th JUNE 2 – 5pm
20% to Childrens Hospice Association Scotland   20% to Marie Curie Cancer Care

65 MONTGOMERY STREET, Eaglesham &
(Mr & Mrs John G Wallace)
Garden set in old village long rig feu within mature tree setting of surrounding gardens and open country. Established for over 25 years on the 700ft contour, with north facing slope it has an arrangement of planting which suits this situation. Plant stall. On B674 through village from East Kilbride to Ayrshire coast.
Admission £1.50 Children over 12 50p
SUNDAY 7th JUNE 2 – 5pm
40% to Eaglesham Old and Carswell Parish Church

BYSTONE MEWS, Clarkston
(Mr & Mrs G C Oldfield)
A much loved garden designed and created by the present owners from uncultivated woodland originally forming part of the boundary of Bystone Estate. Now mature, it contains many interesting shrubs, conifers, simple topiary, perennials and a mini woodland walk. Plant stall. On A726 East Kilbride/Busby near Thortonhall roundabout. Police controlled parking on nearside lanes of dual cariageway.
Admission £1.50 Children free
SUNDAY 19th JULY 2 – 5pm
Private groups by appointment MAY to AUGUST. Tel: (0141) 644 1856
40% to Imperial Cancer Research

GLASGOW BOTANIC GARDENS
(Glasgow City Council)
Visit Scotland's largest collection of filmy ferns. See behind the scenes in the tropical propagation houses where Glasgow's only 'Peepul' tree is grown. Don't miss the famous collections of exotic orchids, ferns, and one of the world's largest begonia collections. Teas and proceeds – Friends of the Botanics. Plant stalls. Corner of Queen Margaret Drive & Great Western Road. Leave motorway at Junction 17, follow signs for A82 Dumbarton.
Admission: Suggested donation £1.00 Children 50p
SUNDAY 16th AUGUST 12 - 4.30pm
Donation to Scotland's Gardens Scheme

GREENBANK HOUSE & GARDEN, Clarkston &
(The National Trust for Scotland)
Within easy reach of city dwellers, this unique walled garden contains a collection of designs of particular interest to suburban gardeners. These include a parterre layout, fountains and a woodland walk, all of which display a wide range of garden plants. Guided garden walk with the Gardening Instructor, Mr Jim May, at 2.30pm. Tours of Greenbank House between 2pm and 5pm. Plant Stall. Clarkston 1 mile.
Bus: Strathclyde no.44D to Mearnskirk or Newton Mearns; alight at Flenders Road.
Admission to Garden £3.00 Children & OAPs £2.00 Family £8.00.
SATURDAY 28th FEBRUARY 11am–5pm
Exhibition in Greenbank House 2–5pm of greenhouse and housegrown orchids by the Glasgow branch of the Scottish Orchid Society. Teas by The Friends of Greenbank.
SATURDAY 9th MAY 11am - 5pm
Embroidery Exhibition by the Renfrewshire branch of The Embroiderers' Guild. Container planting demonstration. Refreshments in the tea room.
40% to The Gardens Fund of The National Trust for Scotland
For other opening details see page 133

INVERMAY, 48 Wellshot Drive, Cambuslang
(Mrs M Robertson)
A plant lovers' garden. Wide variety of unusual bulbs, rock plants, herbaceous plants, shrubs (many named) in a very sheltered, suburban garden. Greenhouse with fuchsias. Something in flower all through the year - a special town garden. Teas. Plant Stall. A730 (East Kilbride) or A749/A724 (Hamilton) from Glasgow. Convenient to M74/M73. Wellshot Drive starts at back of Cambuslang station.
Admission £1.50 Children over 12 50p
APRIL to SEPTEMBER Visitors welcome, please telephone first: 0141 641 1632
40% to Children First

KITTOCH MILL, Carmunnock
(Brigadier & Mrs Howard Jordan)

This waterside and woodland garden contains the National Collection of Hostas in Scotland with over 370 varieties growing in different conditions. Many varieties and species of ligularia are planted out on the river banks and woodland areas. A Japanese-style garden, close to the house featuring a Yatsu-Hashi (zig-zag bridge), leads the visitor over a lacquered bridge into the woodland area. Lots of sunloving plants such as anthemis and geranium are planted out around the terrace. Many other unusual plants are to be seen and the garden is a haven for native flora and fauna. Plant stall with gems from the garden. Please - no dogs. Situated off B759 Busby/Carmunnock. Parking is allowed on far side of road. Admission £1.50

SUNDAYS 21st JUNE & 5th JULY 2 - 5pm
40% to N C C P G (Strathclyde)

SIX FATHOMS, 6 Polnoon Street, Eaglesham   &
(Mr & Mrs A Bewick)

This working garden follows the original tradition of seventeenth century 'strip farming' with self sufficiency the aim. Developed now to contain fruit, vegetables, flowers and two ornamental ponds. Interesting plant stall. B767 Glasgow/Eaglesham. B764 East Kilbride/Eaglesham. Admission £1.50 Children over 12 50p

SUNDAY 2nd AUGUST 2 – 5pm.
By appointment JULY & AUGUST. Tel: 01355 302321
40% to Eastpark Home for Children

TORRANCE DEMONSTRATION GARDEN   & (no disabled toilets)
(East Dunbartonshire Council)

Demonstration and ornamental garden set up by the local authority in 1978 to develop and increase the knowledge of local residents in gardening containing herbaceous perennials, herb garden, water feature and rock garden. Teas. Plant stall. Off A807 Milngavie/Kirkintilloch road at Torrance roundabout. Take B822 into Main Street. left at junction with Campsie Road, first right to School Road.
Admission £1.50 Children 50p

SUNDAY 28th JUNE 2 – 5pm
All takings to Scotland's Gardens Scheme

WHITEMOSS HOUSE, East Kilbride
(Mr & Mrs Albert Heasman)

A garden of one acre, developed over the last 25 years but also containing mature beech, chestnut and sycamore trees. The mixed borders and small woodland garden include a variety of acid loving shrubs and perennials mostly grown from seed or cuttings. Teas. Plant stall. In Whitemoss Recreation Area opposite bowling greens and tennis courts. Enter via the John Wright Sports Centre car park, Calderwood Road and follow signs.
Admission £1.50 Children over 12 50p

SUNDAY 2nd AUGUST 2 - 5pm
40% to Lanarkshire Cancer Care Trust

ISLE OF ARRAN

District Organiser:	**Mrs S C Gibbs,** Dougarie, Isle of Arran KA27 8EB
Hon. Treasurer:	**Mr J Hill,** Bank of Scotland, Brodick, Isle of Arran KA27 8AL

DATES OF OPENING

Dougarie .... Sunday 28 June	2 - 5pm
Brodick Castle & Country Park .... Wednesday 8 July	10am – 5pm
Brodick Castle & Country Park .... Wednesday 19 August	10am – 5pm

BRODICK CASTLE & COUNTRY PARK ♧ (mostly)
(The National Trust for Scotland)
Semi-tropical plants and shrubs. Walled garden. Rock garden. Car park free. Morning
coffee, lunch and tea available in Castle. NTS shop. Brodick 2 miles. Service buses from
Brodick Pier to Castle. Regular sailings from Ardrossan and from Claonaig (Argyll).
Information from Caledonian MacBrayne, Gourock.
Tel: 01475 33755.
Admission to Garden & Country Park £2.40. Children & OAPs £1.60
WEDNESDAYS 8th JULY and 19th AUGUST 10 am - 5 pm
40% to The Gardens Fund of the National Trust for Scotland
For other opening details see page 123

DOUGARIE
(Mr & Mrs S C Gibbs)
Terraced garden in castellated folly. Shrubs, herbaceous borders, traditional kitchen
garden. Tea. Produce stall. Blackwaterfoot 5 miles. Regular ferry sailing from
Ardrossan and from Claonaig (Argyll). Information from Caledonian MacBrayne,
Gourock. Tel: 01475 337355.
Admission £1.50 Children 50p
SUNDAY 28th JUNE 2 - 5pm
40% to Pirnmill Village Hall

KINCARDINE & DEESIDE

District Organiser:	**Mrs J Mackie,** Kirkside of Lochty, Menmuir, by Brechin DD9 6RY
Area Organisers:	**The Hon Mrs J K O Arbuthnott,** Kilternan, Arbuthnott, Laurencekirk AB30 1NA
	Mrs E H Hartwell, Burnigill, Burnside, Fettercairn AB30 1XX
	Dr Frances McCance, House of Strachan, Strachan Banchory AB31 3NN
Hon. Treasurer:	**Mr D S Gauld,** 18 Reed Crescent, Laurencekirk AB30 1EF

DATES OF OPENING

Shooting Greens, Strachan .... 27 April – 10 May by appointment

Shooting Greens, Strachan	Sunday 26 April	2 – 5pm
Inchmarlo House Garden, Banchory	Sunday 7 June	1.30-5pm
Crathes Castle, Banchory	Sunday 21 June	2 – 5.30pm
Drum Castle, Drumoak	Sunday 5 July	1.30 – 5pm
Glassel Lodge, Banchory	Sunday 12 July	2 – 5pm
House of Strachan, Banchory	Sunday 19 July	2 – 5pm
Douneside House, Tarland	Sunday 26 July	2 – 5pm
Glenbervie House, Drumlithie	Sunday 26 July	2 – 5pm
Balmanno, Marykirk..	Sunday 2 August	2 – 5.30pm

BALMANNO, Marykirk, by Laurencekirk ♿ (gravel paths)
(Mr & Mrs Ronald Simson)
A traditional Scottish 18th century walled garden with flower borders and vegetable plots. Splendid views of the Grampians. Home baked teas. Plant stall. Balmanno is three-quarters of a mile north of Marykirk. Turn right at unmarked crossroads, up hill a few hundred yards on right.
Admission £1.50 Children 50p
SUNDAY 2nd AUGUST 2 - 5.30 pm
20% to Macmillan Cancer Ward, Stracathro Hospital   20% to Marykirk Hall Fund

---

CRATHES CASTLE, Banchory ♿
(The National Trust for Scotland)
This historic castle and its gardens are situated near Banchory, in a delightful part of Royal Deeside. Crathes was formerly the home of Sir James & Lady Burnett, whose lifelong interests found expression in the gardens and in one of the best plant collections in Britain. No less than eight colourful gardens can be found within the walled garden. Exhibitions, shop and licensed restaurant. Sale of plants, garden walks, ranger walks, forest walks. Situated off A93, 3 miles east of Banchory, 15 miles west of Aberdeen.
Admission quoted includes castle, garden, estate and use of all facilities. A timed entry system to the castle applies to all visitors to avoid overcrowding in smaller rooms but there is no restriction on time spent inside. Castle tickets can be obtained on arrival.

Admission (combined ticket) £4.80
Children & OAPs £3.20 Family £12.80
SUNDAY 21st JUNE 2 - 5.30 pm
·(Last entry to castle 4.45pm)
40% to The Gardens Fund of The National Trust for Scotland
For other opening details see page 124

DOUNESIDE HOUSE, Tarland ♿
(The MacRobert Trusts)
Ornamental and rose gardens around a large lawn with uninterrupted views to the Deeside Hills and Grampians; large, well-stocked vegetable garden, beech walks and water gardens. Cars free. Tea in house. Plant stall. Ballater and District Pipe Band. Tarland 1½ miles. Route: B9119 towards Aberdeen.
Admission £1.50 Children & OAPs £1.00
SUNDAY 26th JULY 2 - 5 pm
40% to Gardeners' Royal Benevolent Society (Netherbyres Appeal)

DRUM CASTLE, Drumoak, by Banchory ♿
(The National Trust for Scotland)
In the walled garden the Trust has created a unique Garden of Historic Roses, the design of each quadrant representing a different century of gardening. The pleasant parkland contains the 100-acre Old Wood of Drum, coniferous plantations and deciduous woodland, and offers fine views. Marquee teas. Specialist Plant Fair. Special activities for children including tractor rides and Treasure Hunt. Route: 10 miles west of Aberdeen and 8 miles east of Banchory on A93.
Garden & Grounds only £2.00 OAPs & children £1.30
Castle supplement £2.20 Children £1.50 Family ticket £5.30
SUNDAY 5th JULY 1.30 - 5 pm
40% to The Gardens Fund of The National Trust for Scotland
For other opening details see page 124

GLASSEL LODGE, Banchory ♿
(Mr & Mrs M Welsh)
A developing garden containing flowers, kitchen garden and woodland.
Plant stall. 4 miles from A93 west of Banchory take right turn marked Glassel, Torphins, Lumphanan.
Admission £2.00 Children £1.00
SUNDAY 12th JULY 2 - 5pm
40% to Friends of Cruickshank Botanic Garden

GLENBERVIE HOUSE, Drumlithie, Stonehaven
(Mrs C S Macphie)
Nucleus of present day house dates from the 15th century. Additions in 18th and 19th centuries. A traditional Scottish walled garden on a slope with roses, herbaceous and annual borders and fruit and vegetables. One wall is taken up with a fine Victorian conservatory with many varieties of pot plants and climbers on the walls, giving a dazzling display. There is also a woodland garden by a burn with primulas and ferns. Teas. Plant and baking stalls. Drumlithie 1 mile. Garden 1½ miles off A90. NOT SUITABLE FOR WHEELCHAIRS.
Admission £2.00 Children 80p Cars free
SUNDAY 26th JULY 2 - 5 pm
40% to Kincardine & Deeside Guides

HOUSE OF STRACHAN, Strachan, Banchory
(Dr F McCance)

A mature garden of two acres, the grounds of what was Strachan Manse. It slopes south to the River Feugh and has a variety of roses, herbaceous borders and other plants and shrubs. Teas. Plant stall. On B976 on south side in centre of village of Strachan. Admission £2.00.

SUNDAY 19th JULY 2 - 5pm
40% to Friends of Crossroads

INCHMARLO HOUSE GARDEN, Banchory   (limited)
(Skene Enterprises (Aberdeen) Ltd)

An ever changing 5 acre woodland garden within Inchmarlo Continuing Care Retirement Community. Originally planted in the early Victorian era, featuring ancient Scots pines, Douglas firs, yews, beeches and a variety of other trees which form a dramatic background to an early summer riot of mature azaleas and rhododendrons producing a splendour of colour and scents.

Tea, coffee, homebakes - £2.00. From Aberdeen via North Deeside Road on A93 1m west of Banchory, turn right at main gate to Inchmarlo House. Admission £2.00 Children free

SUNDAY 7th JUNE 1.30 - 5pm
40% to British Heart Foundation

SHOOTING GREENS, Strachan, Banchory (limited access)
(Mr & Mrs Donald Stuart-Hamilton)

Medium sized garden, landscaped with local stone, stems from terracing rough moorland near a burn and woodland glen. Short vistas and distant Grampian hills back raised and mixed, erica beds. Row of cairns and two small amphitheatres.

Beyond a chain of ponds, lie short walks by burn and through mixed and beech groves, one to a view point. Forestry Commission walks nearby. CARS PLEASE PARK ALONG PUBLIC ROAD. Route: On east side, near top of north-south Deeside link road between Potarch Hotel (2½m) and Feughside Inn (1m) white stones at drive end; approximately 300 metres from car park for Forestry Commission's own Shooting Greens walks. Admission £1.50 Children 50p

SUNDAY 26th APRIL 2 - 5 pm.   To 10th May by appointment. Tel: 01330 850221.
40% to St Thomas's Church, Aboyne

LOCHABER, BADENOCH & STRATHSPEY

Joint District Organisers:	**Mrs J Drysdale,** Ralia, Newtonmore PH20 1BD
	Mrs J Ramsden, Dalchully, Laggan PH20 1BU
Hon. Treasurer:	**Mrs J Drysdale**

DATES OF OPENING

Ardtornish, Lochaline	Sunday 24 May	2 – 6pm
Ard-Daraich, Ardgour	Sunday 24 May	2 – 5pm
Achnacarry, Spean Bridge	Sunday 31 May	2–5.30pm
Ralia Lodge, Newtonmore	Sunday 28 June	2 – 5pm
Strathmashie House, Newtonmore	Sunday 28 June	2 – 5pm
Aberarder, Kinlochlaggan	Sunday 27 September	2 – 5.30pm
Ardverikie, Kinlochlaggan	Sunday 27 September	2 – 5.30pm

ABERARDER, Kinlochlaggan
(Lady Feilden)
Flower and kitchen garden. Marvellous views down Loch Laggan. Home made teas.
Plant stall. On A86 between Newtonmore and Spean Bridge at east end of Loch Laggan.
Combined admission with ARDVERIKIE £2.00. Children under 12 free
SUNDAY 27th SEPTEMBER 2 - 5.30 pm
40% to Cancer Relief Macmillan Fund

ACHNACARRY, Spean Bridge   &
(Sir Donald & Lady Cameron of Lochiel)
An interesting wild garden in a lovely setting with a profusion of rhododendrons, azaleas
and flowers along the banks of the River Arkaig. A fine Georgian house full of history.
Clan Cameron Museum. Forest walks. Flower stall. Teas in Village Hall 200 yards from
the house. Route: A82 Spean Bridge; left at Commando Memorial marked Gairlochy. At
Gairlochy turn right off B8005. Achnacarry is 7 miles from Spean Bridge.
Admission: House & garden £2.00 Children 50p.
SUNDAY 31st MAY 2 - 5.30pm
40% to Multiple Sclerosis Society (Lochaber)

ARD-DARAICH, Ardgour, by Fort William
(Major David & Lady Edith Maclaren)
Seven acre hill garden, in a spectacular setting, with many fine and uncommon
rhododendrons, an interesting selection of trees and shrubs and a large collection of
camellias, acers and sorbus. Home made teas in house. Cake and plant stall. Route: west
from Fort William, across the Corran Ferry and a mile on the right further west.
Admission £1.50 Children & OAPs 50p
SUNDAY 24th MAY 2 - 5pm
40% to Multiple Sclerosis Society (Fort William branch)

ARDTORNISH, Lochaline, Morvern
(Mrs John Raven)
Garden of interesting mature conifers, rhododendrons, deciduous trees and shrubs set set amidst magnificent scenery. Home made teas in main house 2 – 6pm. Route A884. Lochaline 3 miles.
Admission £2.50 Children free OAPs £1.00
SUNDAY 24th MAY 2 - 6pm.
40% to Morvern Parish Church

ARDVERIKIE, Kinlochlaggan &
(Mrs P Laing & Mrs E T Smyth Osbourne)
Lovely setting on Loch Laggan with magnificent trees. Walled garden with large collection of acers, shrubs and herbaceous. Architecturally interesting house. On A86 between Newtonmore and Spean Bridge - entrance at east end of Loch Laggan, by gate lodge over bridge. Home made teas and plant stall at Aberarder.
Combined admission with ABERARDER £2.00 Children under 12 free
SUNDAY 27th SEPTEMBER 2 - 5.30 pm
40% to Cancer Relief Macmillan Fund

RALIA LODGE, Newtonmore
(Mr & Mrs John Drysdale)
Ralia is a relatively new garden with shrub borders, water garden and views of hills over loch. Home baked teas. Plant stall. A9 to southern Newtonmore turn, 300 yards, fork right, first entrance on left.
Combined admission with STRATHMASHIE HOUSE £2.00 Children free
SUNDAY 28th JUNE 2 – 5pm
20% to British Red Cross Society   20% to the Highland Hospice

---

 # STRATHMASHIE HOUSE, Newtonmore
(Mr & Mrs Geordie Chalmer)
Set in mountainous scenery, this garden is a young bog and herbaceous garden becoming well established. Plant stall. On A86 three miles west of Laggan.
Combined admission with RALIA £2.00 Children free
SUNDAY 28th JUNE 2 – 5pm
20% to British Red Cross Society   20% to the Highland Hospice

MIDLOTHIAN

District Organiser:	**The Hon Mrs C J Dalrymple** OBE, Oxenfoord Mains, Dalkeith EH22 2PF
Area Organisers:	**Mrs George Burnet,** Rose Court, Inveresk
	Mrs S MacMillan, Beechpark House, Broomieknowe, Lasswade EH18 1LN
Joint Hon. Treasurers:	**The Hon Mrs C J Dalrymple** OBE
	Cmdr H Faulkner CVO, Currie Lea, Pathhead EH37 5XB

DATES OF OPENING

Greenfield Lodge, Lasswade .... First Tuesday of each month
  March-September incl. 2 - 5pm
  All year, by appointment
The Mill House, Temple .... Second Wednesday of each month
  April-September incl. 2 - 5pm
Newhall, Carlops .... Tuesday to Thursdays, April - October
  Glen 1 - 5pm. Walled garden 2 - 5pm.

Prestonhall, Pathhead	Sunday 8 March	2 – 5pm
Greenfield Lodge, Lasswade	Tuesday 24 March	2 – 5pm
Oxenfoord Castle, Pathhead	Sunday 12 April	2 - 5.30pm
Prestonhall, Pathhead	Sunday 19 April	2 – 6pm
Penicuik House, Penicuik	Sunday 24 May	2–5.30pm
The Old Parsonage & Brae House,		
Lugton, Dalkeith	Sunday 14 June	2–5.30pm
Whitburgh House, Pathhead	Sunday 12 July	2 – 5pm
Silverburn Village	Sunday 26 July	2 – 5pm
Newhall, Carlops	Sunday 2 August	2 – 6pm
Pentland Plants, Loanhead	Sat & Sun 15/16 August	2 – 5pm
SGS Plant Sale, Oxenfoord Mains,Dalkeith	Saturday 10 October	1 – 4pm
	Sunday 11 October	10.30am–3pm

GREENFIELD LODGE, Lasswade &

(Alan & Helen Dickinson)
A 1½ acre wooded garden with a very wide range of flowering shrubs, unusual
herbaceous plants, ornamental grasses, alpines and bulbs, including the National
Chionodoxa Collection. The garden is designed to give colour and interest throughout
the year: hellebores, cyclamen, aquilegias, meconopsis, eryngiums, dieramas and
gentians are well represented. Early 19th century bow-fronted house with later additions
(not open). Hellebore sales in spring. Parking. No dogs please. Off the Loanhead to
Lasswade road (A768) at the end of Green Lane, which is off Church Road.
Admission £1.50 Careful children free.
First Tuesday of each month MARCH—SEPTEMBER incl. 2 - 5pm
TUESDAY 24th MARCH 2 - 5pm
and throughout the year by appointment., tel. 0131 663 9338 day before proposed visit.
40% to Shelter (Scotland)

THE MILL HOUSE, Temple

(Mrs C F Yannaghas)
A charming riverside garden with botanical interest throughout the year, including
spring flowers, camomile lawn and interesting use of ground cover. A conservation area
within Knights Templar enclave. Cream teas. Temple is 3 miles off A7 on B6372.
Admission £1.50
The second WEDNESDAY of each month APRIL - SEPTEMBER 2 - 5pm
40% to St Mary's Church, Dalkeith

NEWHALL, Carlops   ♿   (Walled garden only)
(Robert Hardy CBE and The Orcome Trust)
Scene of Allan Ramsay's celebrated dramatic poem 'The Gentle Shepherd' and meeting place of the "Worthies", his patrons; glen of the North Esk with "Habbie's How", "Peggy's Pool" and "Craigie Bield". Parkland. Traditional 18th century Scottish walled garden; spring bulbs; mixed borders; shrubs; kitchen garden; lily pool; vine house with sturdy and aged vines. Teas. Some pot plants for sale. **Sorry no dogs.** On A702 Edinburgh/Biggar, exactly half mile after Ninemileburn and 1 mile before Carlops. Gates on left.
APRIL to OCTOBER, Tuesdays, Wednesdays & Thursdays.
Glen: 1 - 5pm; Walled Garden: 2 - 5pm
SUNDAY 2nd AUGUST 2 — 6pm Admission £2.00 Children 50p
40% to Childrens Hospice Association Scotland

The OLD PARSONAGE and BRAE HOUSE, Lugton, Dalkeith
The Old Parsonage (John Stuart Esq)
The garden was laid out in 1845 with herbaceous borders, shrubs and rose beds and extensive views to the south. The large walled garden grows a wide range of vegetables and fruit with a glasshouse for peaches, vines and figs. Teas . Plant stall.
Brae House occupies part of the walled garden with its own flower garden.
Brae House (Mr & Mrs J Stockman)
Large lawn bordered with various shrubs, box hedge, hanging baskets, summer house, large willow tree, statues and surrounded by large flowering trees.
Lugton is ½ mile north of Dalkeith on east side of A68.
Admission £2.00 Children under 12 free
SUNDAY 14th JUNE 2 – 5.30pm
40% to St Mary's Church Restoration Appeal

OXENFOORD CASTLE, near Pathhead   ♿   (partly)
(The Hon Michael Dalrymple)
Extensive grounds with masses of daffodils, some early rhododendrons and new development in sunken garden. The house has been recently renovated and will be open for teas. Easter Egg rolling competition and Easter Egg hunt. Route: A68. Opposite Gorebridge turning ¾ mile north of Pathhead.
Admission £2.00 Children under 12 free
SUNDAY 12th APRIL 2 - 5.30pm
40% to Cranstoun Church

OXENFOORD MAINS, Dalkeith   ♿
SGS BRING AND BUY PLANT SALE
Excellent selection of garden and house plants, many unusual, from private gardens. All reasonably priced. Sale held under cover. 4 miles south of Dalkeith on A68, turn left for one mile on A6093.
Admission free.
SATURDAY 10th OCTOBER 1 – 4pm
SUNDAY 11th OCTOBER 10.30am - 3pm
40% to Cancer Research Campaign

PENICUIK HOUSE, Penicuik &

(Sir John D Clerk Bt)

Landscaped grounds with ornamental lakes, rhododendrons and azaleas. Plant stall. Home baked teas in house. On A766 road to Carlops. Penicuik 2 miles.

Admission £2.00 Children free

SUNDAY 24th MAY 2 – 5.30pm

40% to Marie Curie Flowering of Scotland Appeal

PENTLAND PLANTS, Loanhead &

(David & Hilda Spray)

A display of over 800 varieties of bedding plants form the most northerly trial site in the United Kingdom. View established and new varieties from all over the world. Demonstration gardens, hanging baskets and containers showing use of varieties. Plots laid out by Carolyn Spray of The Beechgrove Garden. Teas. Plant stall.

Just off A701 Edinburgh/Penicuik road near Bilston, one mile from city bypass at Straiton junction.

Admission £2.00 Children free

SATURDAY & SUNDAY 15th & 16th AUGUST 2 – 5pm

40% to Children First

PRESTONHALL, Pathhead &

(Major & Mrs J H Callander)

Set in extensive parkland originally laid out in the 18th century. The mature park trees with their surrounding woodland and wild gardens are a wonderful setting for carpets of snowdrops in March and a profusion of daffodils and rhododendrons in April/May. Many new species of trees have been planted recently. Signed off A68 at Pathhead 25 minutes south east of Edinburgh.

Admission £2.00 (£1.50 in March)

SUNDAY 8th MARCH 2 - 5pm

SUNDAY 19th APRIL 2 - 6pm

20% to Malcolm Sargent Cancer Fund for Children   20% to Crichton Collegiate Church Trust

SILVERBURN VILLAGE & (some gardens)

A selection of village gardens growing at 800ft. Wonderful views and many ideas for growing plants in exposed situations. Home baked teas. Plant stall. Route: A702, 13 miles south of Edinburgh

Admission £2.00 Children free

SUNDAY 26th JULY 2 – 5pm

40% to Romanian Orphanages

WHITBURGH HOUSE, Pathhead &

(Mr & Mrs Alastair Salvesen)

One acre walled kitchen garden mainly planted in last five years. Flowers, fruit, vegetables. Woodland walk. Pond walk. Teas. Plant stall.

Between Pathhead and Fala, east of A68.

Admission £2.00 Children free

SUNDAY 12th JULY 2 – 5pm

40% to Crichton Collegiate Church Trust

MORAY & NAIRN

District Organiser:	**Mrs H D P Brown,** Tilliedivie House, Relugas, Dunphail, Forres IV36 0QL
Hon. Treasurer:	**Mr H D P Brown,** Tilliedivie House, Relugas, Dunphail, Forres IV36 0QL

DATES OF OPENING

Carestown Steading, Deskford	Sunday 7 June	2 - 5pm
Glen Grant Distillery Garden, near Elgin	Saturday 13 June	10am - 5pm
Gordonstoun, Duffus	Sunday 21 June	2 - 5.30pm
Drummuir Castle Garden, by Keith	Sunday 19 July	2 - 5pm

CARESTOWN STEADING, Deskford, Buckie
(Rora Paglieri)
An award winning steading conversion in a three acre rural garden reclaimed from wasteland in 1990 and still developing and maturing. The plants and flowers are native as far as possible and the few exotics have been present in Scotland for many years. The aim is for the gardens to look natural. The one example of manicured gardening is the 90 sq m. of courtyard with knot beds of box in the old Scottish tradition. Vegetable garden, orchard and ponds. Teas by local Guides. Route: East off B9018 Cullen/Keith (Cullen 3m, Keith 9½m). Follow SGS signs towards Milton and Carestown.
Admission £1.50 Children 50p
SUNDAY 7th JUNE 2 - 5pm
All takings to Scotland's Gardens Scheme

DRUMMUIR CASTLE WALLED GARDEN, by Keith
(Mr & Mrs Alex Gordon-Duff)
Traditional walled garden using organic methods to grow fruit, vegetables and herbs. Plant stall. Ice cream. Five miles from Keith and Dufftown on B9014.
Admission £1.50 Children under 12 free
SUNDAY 19th JULY 2 - 5pm
40% to Drummuir Community Association

GLEN GRANT DISTILLERY GARDEN, Rothes, near Elgin ♿ (partly)
(The Chivas and Glenlivet Group)
An award-winning restoration of this delightful Victorian garden created in the glen behind Glen Grant Distillery by Major James Grant, the owner of the distillery. The woodland setting of the enchanting informal garden has been carefully restored to its original Victorian glory. Old woodland walks and log bridges have been rebuilt, the lily pond restored and the lovely mature orchards and rhododendrons have come back into view. The ornamental areas have been replanted with native specimens and plants from America, China and the Himalayas. A visit to the distillery and garden includes exhibitions, audio-visual show about the life of Major Grant and a free dram of Glen Grant pure malt Scotch whisky, which you can choose to enjoy at Major Grant's Dram Pavilion up in the garden if you wish. Route: On A941 Grantown-on-Spey road at north end of Rothes, about 10 miles south of Elgin.
Admission £2.50 Under 18 free
SATURDAY 13th JUNE 10am - 5pm
40% to Grant Hall, Rothes

GORDONSTOUN, Duffus, near Elgin ♿
(The Headmaster, Gordonstoun School)
School grounds; Gordonstoun House (Georgian House of 1775/6 incorporating earlier 17th century house built for 1st Marquis of Huntly) and School Chapel - both open. Unique circle of former farm buildings known as the Round Square. Teas. Entrance off B9012 4 miles from Elgin at Duffus village.
Admission £1.50 Children 50p
SUNDAY 21st JUNE 2 - 5.30pm
All takings to Scotland's Gardens Scheme

PERTH & KINROSS

Joint District Organisers:
Mrs M E Hamilton, Glencarse House, Glencarse PH2 7LF
Mrs Charles Moncrieff, Easter Elcho, Rhynd PH2 8QQ

Area Organisers:
Mrs D J W Anstice, Broomhill, Abernethy PH2 9LQ
Mrs C Dunphie, Wester Cloquhat, Bridge of Cally PH10 7JP
Mrs T J Hope Thomson, High Birches, Fairmount Road, Perth PH2 7AW
Mrs Alastair Leslie, Seasyde House, Errol PH2 7TA
Lady Livesay, Crosshill House, Strathallan, Auchterarder PH3 7LN
Mrs Colin Maitland Dougall, Dowhill, Kelty, Fife KY4 0HZ
The Hon Mrs Ranald Noel Paton, Easter Dunbarnie, Bridge of Earn PH2 9ED
Mrs Athel Price, Urlar Farm, Aberfeldy PH15 2EW

Hon. Treasurer:
Mrs J Bell, Greenwood, Kinfauns, Perth PH2 7JZ

DATES OF OPENING

Ardvorlich, Lochearnhead .... 10 May - 7 June inclusive   2 – 6pm
Bolfracks, Aberfeldy .... 1 April – 31 October   10am – 6pm
Cluny House, Aberfeldy .... 1 March – 31 October   10am – 6pm
Drummond Castle Gardens, Muthill ... May – October   2 – 6pm, last entrance 5pm
Scone Palace, Perth .... 10 April–12 October   9.30–5.15, last entrance 4.45
Wester Dalqueich, Carnbo .... By appt: groups of 10 or more, late May– August

Meikleour House, by Blairgowrie	Sunday 12 April	2 - 5pm
Cleish Gardens, Kinross	Sunday 26 April	2 – 5pm
Kennacoil House, Dunkeld	Sunday 26 April	2 – 6pm
Glendoick, by Perth	Sunday 3 May	2 – 5pm
Branklyn, Perth	Sunday 10 May	9.30am – sunset
Meikleour House, by Blairgowrie	Sunday 10 May	2 - 5pm
Glendoick, by Perth	Sunday 17 May	2 – 5pm
Stobhall, by Perth	Sunday 24 May	2 – 6pm
Dowhill, Cleish	Sunday 7 June	2 – 5pm
Meikleour House, by Blairgowrie	Sunday 7 June	2 - 5pm
Branklyn, Perth	Sunday 14 June	9.30am – sunset
Cloquhat Gardens, Bridge of Cally	Sunday 14 June	2 – 6pm
Rossie Priory, Inchture	Sunday 21 June	2 – 6pm
Pitcarmick, Bridge of Cally	Sunday 28 June	2 - 6pm
The Bank House, Glenfarg	Sunday 12 July	2 – 6pm
Easter Elcho, Rhynd	Sunday 19 July	2 – 5pm
Balvarran, Enochdu	Sunday 26 July	2 – 6pm
Boreland, Killin	Sunday 26 July	2–5.30pm
Blairgowrie & Rattray Gardens	Sunday 2 August	1 – 6pm
Drummond Castle Gardens, Muthill	Sunday 2 August	2 – 6pm
Cluniemore, Pitlochry	Sunday 9 August	2 – 5pm
Megginch Castle, Errol	Sunday 9 August	2 – 5pm
Bonskeid House, near Pitlochry	Sunday 20 September	2 – 5pm
Meikleour House, by Blairgowrie	Sunday 18 October	2 - 5pm
Stobhall, by Perth	Sunday 25 October	2 - 6pm
Stobhall, by Perth	Sunday 1 November	2 - 6pm

ARDVORLICH, Lochearnhead
(Mr & Mrs Sandy Stewart)
Beautiful glen with rhododendrons (species and many hybrids) grown in wild conditions amid oaks and birches. Gum boots advisable when wet.
On south Lochearn road 3m from Lochearnhead, 4½m from St Fillans.
Admission £1.50 Children under 12 free
10th MAY to 7th JUNE incl. 2 - 6pm
40% to St Columba's Hospice

BALVARRAN, Enochdu, Blairgowrie
(Mr & Mrs Robin Stormonth-Darling)
Started in 1990. Glorious glen setting with terrific views. Basically woodland
with formal area and lochan/water garden. Vegetable garden also open. Teas. Plant
stall. Route: on A924 between Pitlochry and Bridge of Cally, one mile west of
Kirkmichael. No dogs please.
Admission £2.00 Children under 12 50p
SUNDAY 26th JULY 2 – 6pm
40% to Leonard Cheshire Foundation in Scotland

THE BANK HOUSE, Glenfarg   ꝺ (mostly)
(Mr & Mrs C B Lascelles)
A large garden (for the centre of a village) in two parts. Behind the house a tunnel of
apple trees leads from a stone-paved area into the main garden of shrubs and herbaceous
plants, many of them unusual. Pond, fountains, sculpture; raised-bed vegetable system,
organic methods throughout; advanced compost-making equipment. Across the road,
water cascades down steps to a further garden with a large Yin-Yang bed, from where a
bridge crosses the stream to a field in which a wildlife pond has been created and
ornamental trees planted. Gardening's ultimate challenge - a wildflower meadow - at the
furthest end. Teas in Village Hall. Alas, no plant stall. Situated 50 yards down side road
by Glenfarg Hotel.
Admission £2.00 Children free
SUNDAY 12th JULY 2 – 6pm
40% to The Phoenix Prison Trust

BLAIRGOWRIE & RATTRAY   ꝺ (partly)
The "Blair in Bloom" Committee would like to invite you to visit some colourful
prizewinning town gardens of varying sizes. Teas and Plant Stalls. Maps and tickets
available from the Tourist Information Centre, Wellmeadow, Blairgowrie. No dogs,
except guide dogs, please.
Admission £2.00 Accompanied children under 12 free
SUNDAY 2nd AUGUST 1 - 6pm
40% to Local Registered Charities

BOLFRACKS, Aberfeldy
(Mr J D Hutchison CBE)
Garden overlooking the Tay valley. Walled garden with borders of trees, shrubs and
perennials. Burn garden with rhododendrons, azaleas, primulas, meconopsis, etc. in
woodland setting. Masses of bulbs in spring. Good autumn colour. No dogs please.
Limited range of plants for sale. Route: 2 miles west of Aberfeldy on A827. White gates
and Lodge on left of road. Not suitable for wheelchairs.
Admission £2.00 Children under 16 free
DAILY 1st APRIL to 31st OCTOBER 10 am - 6 pm
Donation to Scotland's Gardens Scheme

'BY APPOINTMENT' gardens welcome visitors outwith normal opening times

— for details see pages 10–12

BONSKEID HOUSE, near Pitlochry
(YMCA Scottish National Council)
The house, formerly the property of George Freeland Barbour, has been run as a holiday
and conference centre by the YMCA since 1921. The house and grounds
(38 acres) were sited in 1800 by Alexander Stewart to take advantage of the dramatic
views across the River Tummel, and for visitors to experience the romanticism of a
baronial residence in a wild woodland setting. Woodland walks, some steep paths,
wandering amongst mature exotic specimen trees and ponticum rhododendrons. After
suffering many years of neglect, the grounds have now benefited from 36 months of an
ongoing reclamation project. Flower beds under construction, walled garden reclaimed,
lovely autumn colours. Teas. Route: A9 Killiecrankie exit, 4 miles along B8019 Tummel
Bridge road, on left hand side.
Admission £1.50 Children 50p
SUNDAY 20th SEPTEMBER 2 – 5pm
20% to YMCA   20% to the Scottish Wildlife Trust

BORELAND, Killin &
(Mrs Angus Stroyan)
A varied garden but with border the main feature. Very pretty walk along river leading
to arboretum. Teas. Plant stall. Route: through Killin, first turning left over bridge after
Bridge of Lochay Hotel. House approx. 2m on left.
Admission £1.50 Children over 12 50p
SUNDAY 26th JULY 2 - 5.30pm
40% to Cancer Research (Killin branch)

BRANKLYN, Perth
(The National Trust for Scotland)
Famed for its alpines, meconopsis and autumn colour, this garden, created by the late Mr
& Mrs Renton, provides year-round inspiration for visitors. Tea and coffee. On A85
Perth/Dundee road.
Admission £2.40 Children & OAPs £1.60 Family £6.40
SUNDAY 10th MAY and SUNDAY 14th JUNE 9.30 am - sunset
40% to The Gardens Fund of The National Trust for Scotland
For other opening details see page 122

 # CLEISH GARDENS, Kinross &

Cleish Castle (Mr & Mrs S Miller)   **Cleish House** (Mr & Mrs D Erskine)

Mawmill House (Mr & Mrs A Whitehead)   **The Manse** (Rev & Mrs MacLeod)

Boreland House (Mr & Mrs N Kilpatrick)
The castle garden is being re-constructed and woodland cleared. Two of the other
gardens are four years old, created out of fields, and there are two small, mature gardens.
Teas. Plant stall. No dogs please. Route: Junction 5 of M90, take B9097 towards Crook
of Devon, Cleish two miles.
Admission £2.00 includes all five gardens
SUNDAY 26th APRIL 2 – 5pm
40% to Children First

CLOQUHAT GARDENS, Bridge of Cally ♿ (partly)
Cloquhat. (Colonel Peter Dunphie CBE)
Fine views down to river. Azaleas, rhododendrons, shrubs. Woodland and burnside gardens. Terrace with rock plants. Walled garden.
Wester Cloquhat. (Brigadier & Mrs Christopher Dunphie)
Small garden started in 1989. Splendid situation. Several mixed borders with wide variety of shrubs and herbaceous plants. Heather bank. Teas and plant stall. No dogs please. Turn off A93 just north of Bridge of Cally and follow yellow signs one mile.
Admission to both gardens £2.00 Children 50p
SUNDAY 14th JUNE 2 - 6 pm
20% to Leonard Cheshire Foundation in Scotland   20% to SSAFA Forces Help

CLUNIEMORE, Pitlochry ♿
(Major Sir David & Lady Butter)
Water garden, rock garden. Woodlands in beautiful setting. Shrubs, herbaceous borders, annual border and roses. Plant stall. Tea, biscuits and ice cream.
Parties by appointment any time. On A9 Pitlochry bypass.
Admission £2.00 Children under 16 free
SUNDAY 9th AUGUST 2 - 5pm
40% to The Pushkin Prizes in Scotland

CLUNY HOUSE, Aberfeldy
(Mr J & Mrs W Mattingley)
Woodland garden with many specimen trees, shrubs and rhododendrons, with extensive views of Strathtay to Ben Lawers. An outstanding collection of primulas, meconopsis, nomocharis, cardiocrinums and other Himalayan plants. Autumn colour. Plant stall. No dogs please. 3½ miles from Aberfeldy on Weem to Strathtay road.
Admission £2.00 Children under 16 free
DAILY 1st MARCH to 31st OCTOBER 10 am - 6 pm
Donation to Scotland's Gardens Scheme

DOWHILL, Cleish
(Mr & Mrs C Maitland Dougall)
 A garden of interest to all those who like water and ponds. Started 10 years ago, there are now seven ponds linked by pipe and burn, set off by a backdrop of wonderful mature trees. Rhododendrons, primulas and blue poppies. Woodland walk to ruins of Dowhill Castle. Teas. Plant stall. Musical entertainment by Kinross High School children. Route: ¾ mile off M90, exit 5, towards Crook of Devon.
Admission £2.00 Children 50p
SUNDAY 7th JUNE 2 - 5pm
40% to R N L I Crew Training Appeal, Kinghorn

DRUMMOND CASTLE GARDENS, Crieff &

(Grimsthorpe & Drummond Castle Trust Ltd)

The gardens of Drummond Castle were originally laid out in 1630 by John Drummond, 2nd Earl of Perth. In 1830 the parterre was changed to an Italian style. One of the most interesting features is the multi-faceted sundial designed by John Mylne, Master Mason to Charles I. The formal garden is said to be one of the finest in Europe and is the largest of its type in Scotland. Open daily May to October 2 - 6 pm (last entrance 5 pm). Entrance 2 miles south of Crieff on Muthill road (A822).

Admission £3.00 OAPs £2.00 Children £1.00

SUNDAY 2nd AUGUST 2 - 6 pm. Teas, raffle, entertainments & stalls.

40% to British Limbless Ex-Servicemen's Association

EASTER ELCHO, Rhynd, by Perth   &

(Captain & Mrs Charles Moncrieff)

The garden was redesigned and planted 8 years ago with mixed shrub borders, a vegetable garden and a walk through an old orchard, now planted with shrub roses and a yellow border. The walk round takes you to the Mill Pond which is still being established with shrubs, trees and damp-loving plants. This leads on to the recently restored 15th century doocot which lies adjacent to Elcho Castle (open to visitors). Plant stall. Home made teas. Route: Exit 9 from M90, through Bridge of Earn. Turn right after crossing the Earn, signed to Rhynd and Elcho castle. Yellow signs in Rhynd village. No dogs please.

Admission £2.00 Children under 12 free

SUNDAY 19th JULY 2 – 5pm

40% to Rhynd Church

GLENDOICK, Perth & (partly)

(Mr & Mrs Peter Cox & family)

Georgian house about 1746 (not open). A lot of replanting in the area by the house is taking place. Walled garden is a mixture of commercial nursery, wall shrubs, trained fruit trees and herbaceous borders. The woodland garden, on the slope above, has meandering paths through the famous rhododendrons and magnolias and many other shrubs and trees. These are complemented by many naturalised herbaceous and wild flowers which make it an enchanting walk. Nursery also open. No dogs please. Refreshments at garden centre 9.30am–5pm. On A90 Perth/Dundee road.

Admission £2.00 Children under 5 free

SUNDAYS 3rd & 17th MAY 2 - 5 pm

40% to World Wide Fund for Nature

KENNACOIL HOUSE, Dunkeld

(Mrs Walter Steuart Fothringham)

Informal to wild garden with herbaceous border, shrubs, rhododendrons, daffodils and spring bulbs on hillside with exceptional view. Teas. Plant stall. No dogs please. Dunkeld 3 miles, off Crieff road A822.

Admission £2.00

SUNDAY 26th APRIL 2 - 6 pm

40% to Scottish European Aid

MEGGINCH CASTLE, Errol ♿
(Captain Drummond of Megginch & Baroness Strange)
15th century turreted castle (not open) with Gothic courtyard and pagoda dovecote. 1,000 year old yews and topiary. Colourful annual border in walled garden. Astrological garden. Home made teas. Plant stall. Memorabilia from "Rob Roy" filmed in the courtyard. Water garden. On A85 between Perth (9½m) and Dundee (12m). Look for Lodge on south side of road.
Admission £2.00 Children free
SUNDAY 9th AUGUST 2 - 5 pm
40% to All Saints Church, Glencarse

MEIKLEOUR HOUSE, by Blairgowrie ♿ (with assistance)
(The Marquis of Lansdowne)
Water and woodland garden on the banks of the River Tay. Fine trees, specie rhododendrons and lovely autumn colours. No dogs please. Entrance to water and woodland garden 300 yards from car parks. Enter via Meikleour Lodge, 5 miles south of Blairgowrie off A93 at its junction with the Stanley/Kinclaven Bridge road.
Admission £1.50 Children free
SUNDAYS 12th APRIL, 10th MAY, 7th JUNE, 18th OCTOBER 2 – 5pm
40% to R N I B (Scotland)

PITCARMICK, Bridge of Cally ♿
(Sir Michael & Lady Nairn)
Informal Highland garden set on the banks of the River Ardle. A good mixture of bulbs, shrubs, herbaceous plants and acers, including the log cabin of Wester Pitcarmick built in 1988. Garden planted with many sorbus leading up the hill to the arboretum originally established in the 1920s (20 mins walk). Teas. Plant stall. Situated on A924 between Kirkmichael and Bridge of Cally.
Admission £2.00 Children under 12 free
SUNDAY 28th JUNE 2 – 6pm
40% to Cystic Fibrosis Holdiday Fund for Children

ROSSIE PRIORY, Inchture ♿
(The Hon Mrs Best)
Extensive grounds include terraced lawns with views over the cricket pitch to the distant hills of Fife. New shrub and rose borders. Herbaceous borders. Walled garden. Water garden. Re-established rhododendron and garden walks. Lovely woodland walks to burn and waterfall. Fine trees. Tea and biscuits. Plant stall. Route: from A90 Perth/Dundee take B953 signed to Abernyte. After two-thirds of a mile, turn first right. No dogs please.
Admission £2.00 Children 50p
SUNDAY 21st JUNE 2 – 6pm
40% to Childrens Hospice Association Scotland

SCONE PALACE, Perth   ♿
(The Earl of Mansfield)
Extensive and well laid out grounds and a magnificent pinetum dating from 1848; there is a Douglas Fir raised from the original seed sent from America in 1824. The Woodland Garden has attractive walks amongst the rhododendrons and azaleas and leads into the Monks' Playgreen and Friar's Den of the former Abbey of Scone. The Palace of Scone lies adjacent to the Moot Hill where the Kings of Scots were crowned. Full catering by the Palace staff. Adventure playground. Special rates for season tickets and parties. Route A93. Perth 2 miles.
Admission: Palace & Grounds: £5.20 Children £3.00 OAPs £4.40 Family £16.00
Grounds only: £2.60 Children £1.50
FRIDAY 10th APRIL to MONDAY 12th OCTOBER 9.30am – 5.15pm daily
(last entry 4.45pm)
Donation to Scotland's Gardens Scheme

STOBHALL, by Perth   ♿
(The Earl of Perth)
Group of early and mediaeval buildings, including castle and chapel with painted ceiling, on ridge high above River Tay. Site of dwelling houses since 14th century, associated with two Queens of Scotland. Early topiary garden, also wild garden and walk in woodland glen. Terrace walk below castle. 1½m north of Guildtown on A93 midway between Perth and Blairgowrie.
Admission to gardens and chapel £2.00 Children £1.00
SUNDAY 24th MAY 2 - 6pm
40% to the Innerpeffray Library
SUNDAYS 25th OCTOBER & 1st NOVEMBER 2 – 6pm
A walk round the policies to see the autumn colouring.
20% to Innerpeffray Library 20% to Help the Hospices

WESTER DALQUEICH, Carnbo   ♿ (partly)
(Mr & Mrs D S Roulston)
A plantsman's garden of two acres by the Ochil Hills, 600ft above sea level. A wide range of interesting herbaceous and rock plants, shrubs with informal planting in the glades. No dogs, except guide dogs please. Carnbo village is west of Milnathort. Leave A91 near Carnbo village and travel north for ½ mile.
Admission £2.00
OPEN BY APPOINTMENT for groups of 10 or more, late MAY, JUNE, JULY and AUGUST. Please telephone beforehand: 01577 840229
40% to Strathcarron Hospice, Denny

RENFREW & INVERCLYDE

Joint District Organisers:	**Mrs J R Hutton,** Auchenclava, Finlaystone, Langbank PA14 6TJ
	Mrs Daphne Ogg, Nittingshill, Kilmacolm PA13 4SG
Area Organisers:	**Lady Denholm,** Newton of Bell Trees, Lochwinnoch PA12 4JL
	Mr J Wardrop, St Kevins, Victoria Road, Paisley PA2 9PT
Hon. Treasurer:	**Mrs Jean Gillan,** 28 Walkerston Avenue, Largs KA30 8ER

DATES OF OPENING

Crossways, by Bishopton .... First Sunday March–September   1–5pm
31 Kings Road, Elderslie .... By appointment, April to June

Ardgowan, Inverkip	Sunday 15 February	2 – 5pm
Finlaystone, Langbank	Sunday 19 April	2 – 5pm
Renfrew Council Central Nursery	Sat & Sun 16/17 May	1 – 5pm
Carruth Plant Sale, Bridge of Weir	Sunday 31 May	2 – 5pm
Middlepenny Gardens, Langbank	Sunday 14 June	2 – 5pm
Lunderston, Ardgowan	Sunday 28 June	2 – 5pm
6 The Grove, Bridge of Weir	Sunday 12 July	2 – 5pm
Greenock Gardens	Sunday 19 July	1.30–5.30pm
Uplawmoor Gardens	Sunday 2 August	2–5.30pm
Johnstone & Kilbarchan Gardens	Sunday 16 August	2 – 5pm

6 THE GROVE, Bridge of Weir
(Mr & Mrs J R Gilchrist)
Small garden packed with plants, mainly herbaceous and shrubs specialising in variegated and coloured foliage including grasses and bonsai. New roof garden. Plant stall and teas at Menteith, Eldin Place. Take Kilbarchan road out of Bridge of Weir, right into Ranfurly Road, left into Eldin Place - The Grove is just round the corner.
Admission £1.50 Children & OAPs £1.00
SUNDAY 12th JULY 2 – 5pm
40% to Cancer Research

31 KINGS ROAD, Elderslie
(Dr & Mrs John Gibb)
A plantsman's garden in a small space (20 yds by 15 yds). Small trees and shrubs underplanted with primulae, meconopsis and spring bulbs. Guided stroll. Plant stall. A737 from Paisley/Johnstone, turn left into Kings Road just before traffic lights at Thorn junction. Garden on left near top of road.
Admission £1.50 Children free
By Appointment APRIL, MAY & JUNE Tel: 01505 320480
All takings to Scotland's Gardens Scheme

ARDGOWAN, Inverkip ♿ (not advisable if wet)
(Sir Houston and Lady Shaw-Stewart)
Woodland walks carpeted with snowdrops. (Strong footwear advised). Tea in house.
Snowdrop stall, home baking and plant stall. Souvenirs. Inverkip 1½ miles. Glasgow/
Largs buses in Inverkip.
Admission £1.00 Children under 10 free
SUNDAY 15th FEBRUARY 2 - 5 pm
40% to the Leonard Cheshire Foundation in Scotland

CARRUTH, Bridge of Weir ♿
(Mr & Mrs Charles Maclean)
PLANT SALE. Big selection of herbaceous, herbs and shrubs etc., in lovely country
setting. Beautiful trees and many different rhododendrons. Teas. Woodland walking.
Access from B786 Kilmacolm/Lochwinnoch road.
Admission £1.50
SUNDAY 31st MAY 2 - 5pm
40% to Cancer Relief Macmillan Fund

CROSSWAYS, by Bishopton ♿
(James Mackie & Gerald Lloyd-Gray)
A new garden of 13 years, level and just over one acre. Mainly rhododendrons and
azaleas. 80ft lily pond, bamboos, gunnera and 'walk-in' cloche. Tea and biscuits. Plant
stall. Roadside car parking. From Bishopton proceed up hill following Formakin signs.
Crossways is first on left and the first of three houses known as 'The Three Bears', prior to
Bishopton cemetery.
Admission £1.50 OAPs £1.00 Accompanied children free
FIRST SUNDAY MARCH – SEPTEMBER incl. 1 – 5pm
40% to Erskine Hospital

FINLAYSTONE, Langbank ♿
(Mr & Mrs George G MacMillan)
Historic connection with John Knox and Robert Burns. Richly varied gardens with
unusual plants overlooking the Clyde. A profusion of daffodils and early
rhododendrons. Waterfalls & pond. Woodland walks with play and picnic areas.
'Eye-opener' centre with shop. Celtic and Dolly Mixture exhibitions. Ranger service.
Plant stall. Teas in the Celtic Tree in the walled garden.
Admission to House: £1.50 Children & OAPs £1.00. Langbank station 1 mile.
On A8 west of Langbank, 10 minutes by car west of Glasgow Airport.
Admission £2.40 Children & OAPs £1.40
SUNDAY 19th APRIL 2 - 5 pm
20% to Quarrier's Village 20% to Erskine Hospital

GREENOCK GARDENS (All located at the west end of Greenock)
6 The Craigs, Newark Street (Mr & Mrs I Marr)
Sizeable, sloping garden. Tender and unusual plants, bog garden. Plant stall.
2 The Craigs, Newark Street (Mrs McCallum)
A pretty enclosed town garden
14 Stoneleigh Road (Mr & Mrs W McVey)
A steep, intensively planted exuberant garden. Plant stall.
16 Stoneleigh Road (Mr & Mrs D Lee)
A simple, uncluttered garden with paving, lawns and shrubs
131 Newton Street (Mr & Mrs S J Hendry)
Newly landscaped and replanted garden with good use of water features. Teas.
La Casita, 21 Finnart Road & (Mr & Mrs J M P Thompson)
New, small, secluded garden with patio and tubs. Teas.
50 Rankin Street (Mr & Mrs Fred Ball)
A colourful little gem of a garden.
A78 to Greenock and approach from Campbell or Robertson Streets. Watch out for
yellow signs. Tickets and maps at all gardens. Admission £2.50 includes all gardens.
SUNDAY 19th JULY 1.30 – 5.30pm
40% between Ardgowan Hospice and Sense Scotland

JOHNSTONE & KILBARCHAN GARDENS & (all)
Fäilte, 11 Auchengrange Avenue, Johnstone (Mr & Mrs D McManus)
Small garden with heathers, herbaceous border, ornamental fish pond. Plant stall and
woodturned articles. Route: leave M8 at St James interchange heading south on A737
signed Irvine. At Kilbarchan exit turn left at mini roundabout. At next roundabout turn
right on to B787, soon first left and left again. Five minutes by car to:
6 Langside Park, Kilbarchan (Mr & Mrs A Deans)
Cottage garden style with rockery and shrubs to give year round colour. Also herbs, fruit
and vegetables.
10 Langside Park, Kilbarchan (Mrs A Wilkinson)
Three tiered garden with herbaceous borders, summer bedding, displays on both patios,
assorted climbers and rockery. Teas. Tickets available at all gardens.
Admission £2.00 includes all three gardens
SUNDAY 16th AUGUST 2 – 5pm
40% between Arthritis Research and St Vincent's Hospice, Howwood

---

LUNDERSTON, Ardgowan, Inverkip &
(Dr J L Kinloch)
A six acre garden at sea level. Surrounding the House, shrubs, lawns, herbaceous
borders and rose beds make a pleasant foreground to the view of the Firth of Clyde
beyond. To one side of the house there is a kitchen garden which combines with a
spacious greenhouse to provide fresh vegetables year round. The latest development lies
beyond this and comprises extensive sweeps of grass bordered by impressive plantings
of over two thousand roses. Plant stall. Teas. Enter Ardgowan at North Lodge and
follow signs.
Admission £1.50 Children over 10 & OAPs £1.00
SUNDAY 28th JUNE 2 - 5pm
20% to Ardgowan Hospice 20% to Erskine Hospital

MIDDLEPENNY GARDENS, Langbank
Four very different steep gardens, with wonderful views of the Clyde estuary and the 'hills of the north' beyond.

51 Middlepenny Road (Fiona & Gordon Guthrie)
Good views, pond and vegetable patch
Birkenshaw, 24 Middlepenny Road (Marion & Bill Dornan)
Approx. one acre with mature trees and rhododendrons.
25 Middlepenny Place (Margaret Beveridge)
Interesting and colourful small cottage garden
19 Middlepenny Place (James & Mary Bonner)
Small garden, still developing with pleasant outlook.
Tickets, parking, Plant Stall and Teas at the Village Hall in Middlepenny Road. Route: M8/A8, ten mins. west of Glasgow Airport, take exit to Langbank, turn into Middlepenny Road by church and follow signs.
Admission £2.00 includes all four gardens
SUNDAY 14th JUNE 2 – 5pm
20% to Scottish Society for the Prevention of Cruelty to Animals
20% to Childrens Hospice Association Scotland

RENFREWSHIRE COUNCIL CENTRAL NURSERY, Hawkhead Road, Paisley &
(Renfrewshire Council)
Three-quarters of an acre under glass, intensively cropped, associated with Open Day demonstrations. Exhibitions of related crafts, countryside interpretation etc. Entertainments etc. Tea served in marquee. Plant stall.
Admission £1.50 Children & OAPs 75p
SATURDAY & SUNDAY 16th & 17th MAY 1 - 5 pm
40% to Erskine Hospital

UPLAWMOOR GARDENS
A group of varied gardens at about 450ft above sea level, off the A736 Glasgow to Irvine road, 5m southwest of Barrhead and 2m north of Lugton. When approaching from Barrhead, the gardens are, in turn:
Woodlands, Birchwood Road. & partly (Mr & Mrs J West)
A moderately sized garden with mixed border, old fashioned roses, and fuchsias, a "cottage garden" and small woodland garden.
 # Church Memorial Garden, Caldwell Parish Church, Neilston Road
37 Neilston Road & (Mr & Mrs D Ritson) Relatively young garden with wide variety of flowering shrubs, herbaceous plants and water feature.
11 Neilston Road (Miss A D Baker) A sloping garden with shrubs, perennials, annual flowers and vegetables which can be viewed along with its neighbouring gardens.
#Greystones, Lochlibo Road (Mr & Mrs J Gauld) A flower garden, a vegetable garden and herb garden bordered with herbaceous plants.
Teas at Caldwell Parish Church, Neilston Road. Plant stall at Woodlands. Tickets available at all gardens.
Admission £2.00 to include all gardens   Accompanied children under 14 free
SUNDAY 2nd AUGUST 2 - 5.30pm
40% to Cancer Relief Macmillan Fund

ROSS, CROMARTY, SKYE & INVERNESS

District Organiser:	**Lady Lister-Kaye,** House of Aigas, Beauly IV4 7AD
Area Organiser:	**Mrs Robin Fremantle,** Fannyfield, Evanton IV16 9XA
Hon. Treasurer:	**Mr Kenneth Haselock,** 2 Tomich, Strathglass, by Beauly IV4 7LZ

DATES OF OPENING

Abriachan Garden Nursery	February – November 9am–dusk
Attadale, Strathcarron	Easter-end October, not Suns. 10–5pm
Brin House, Strathnairn	1 & 2, 8–16 & 21–23 August 10.30–5pm
Clan Donald, Isle of Skye	Daily all year
Coiltie, Divach, Drumnadrochit	Daily 16 May – 31 July 12 – 7pm
Dunvegan Castle, Isle of Skye	23 March – 31 October 10am-5pm
	November – March 11am–3.30pm
Glamaig, Braes, Isle of Skye	Daily Easter – mid-September
Leckmelm Shrubbery & Arboretum	Daily 1 April – 30 Sept 10am– 6pm
Sea View, Dundonnell	May to September or by appt.
Tournaig, Poolewe	By appointment

Inverewe, Poolewe	Saturday 25 April	9.30am – 9pm
Allangrange, Munlochy	Sunday 10 May	2 – 5.30pm
Tournaig, Poolewe	Wednesday 27 May	2pm
House of Gruinard, by Laide	Wednesday 3 June	2 – 5pm
Attadale, Strathcarron	Saturday 6 June	2 – 6pm
Brahan, Dingwall	Sunday 7 June	2 – 5.30pm
Kyllachy, Tomatin	Sunday 7 June	2 – 5pm
Achnashellach Station House	Fri & Sat 12/13 June	10am–6pm
Allangrange, Munlochy	Sunday 14 June	2 – 5.30pm
Lochalsh Woodland Garden, Balmacara	Saturday 20 June	1 – 5pm
House of Gruinard, by Laide	Wednesday 24 June	2 – 5pm
Kilcoy Castle, Muir of Ord	Sunday 5 July	2 - 6pm
Allangrange, Munlochy	Sunday 12 July	2 – 5.30pm
House of Aigas & Field Centre	Sunday 19 July	2 – 5.30pm
The Hydroponicum, Achiltibuie	Sunday19 July	10am – 6pm
Inverewe, Poolewe	Sunday 26 July	9.30am – 9pm
Kyllachy, Tomatin	Sunday 26 July	2 – 5pm
House of Gruinard, by Laide	Wednesday 5 August	2 – 5pm
Tournaig, Poolewe	Wednesday 12 August	2pm
The Hydroponicum, Achiltibuie	Sunday 16 August	10am – 6pm

ABRIACHAN GARDEN NURSERY, Loch Ness Side
(Mr & Mrs Davidson)
An outstanding garden. Over 2 acres of exciting plantings, with winding paths through native woodlands. Seasonal highlights - hellebores, primulas, meconopsis, hardy geraniums and colour themed summer beds. Views over Loch Ness.
Admission by collecting box. Adults £1.50
FEBRUARY to NOVEMBER 9 am - dusk

ACHNASHELLACH STATION HOUSE
(Mr & Mrs P H Hainsworth)
A one acre garden started in 1975 by a plant enthusiast. Part old railway siding, part winding paths through a wild garden with a very wide range of plants, especially ferns, and habitats. Fine mountain scenery and forest walks nearby. 9 miles east of Lochcarron. Cars take forest road (1 mile, courtesy Forestry Commission) 300 yards EAST of railway bridge over A890, or walk 400 yards from telephone box half mile WEST of railway bridge.
Admission £1.50
FRIDAY & SATURDAY 12th & 13th JUNE 10am - 6pm
40% to Association for the Protection of Rural Scotland

ALLANGRANGE, Munlochy, Black Isle &
(Major Allan Cameron)
A formal and a wild garden containing flowering shrubs, trees and plants, especially rhododendrons, shrub roses, meconopsis and primulas. Plants for sale. Exhibition of botanical paintings by Elizabeth Cameron. Teas in house. Inverness 5 miles. Signposted off A9.
Admission £1.50
SUNDAYS 10th MAY, 14th JUNE and 12th JULY 2 - 5.30 pm
40% to Highland Hospice

ATTADALE, Strathcarron
(Mr & Mrs Ewen Macpherson)
Twenty acres of old rhododendrons, azaleas and unusual shrubs in woodland setting with views of Skye and the sea. Water gardens and sunken formal garden. Restored Victorian vegetable and herb garden. On A890 between Strathcarron and South Strome.
Admission £2.00 Children & OAPs £1.00
EASTER – end OCTOBER 10am - 5pm. Closed Sundays
Donation to Scotland's Gardens Scheme
SATURDAY 6th JUNE 2 - 6pm Teas in house. Plant stall.
40% to Howard Doris Development Fund

BRAHAN, Dingwall
(Mr & Mrs A Matheson)
Wild garden, dell with azaleas and rhododendrons. Arboretum with labelled trees and river walk. Home made teas in house. Maryburgh 1½ miles. Take road west from Maryburgh roundabout.
Admission £1.50 Children free
SUNDAY 7th JUNE 2 - 5.30 pm
40% to Highland Hospice

BRIN HOUSE, Strathnairn, by Inverness   ♿

(Mrs J F Furness)

19th century walled garden with interesting plants. Parkland and semi-rough woodland walks. Car parking and dog walking facilities. On B851 Inverness/Fort Augustus, approx. 5 miles from A9 turn off and 20 miles from Fort Augustus.

Admission £1.50 Children under 16 free

1st & 2nd, 8th – 16th & 21st – 23rd AUGUST   10.30am–5pm

40% to Children First

CLAN DONALD VISITOR CENTRE   ♿

The "Garden of Skye" nestles in a sheltered corner of Skye's Sleat peninsula. The 40 acres of woodland garden are based around a 19th century collection of exotic trees. Much of the garden has been restored, displaying plants from around the world. New features include the ponds, rockery, herbaceous borders and terrace walk. Disabled facilities: toilet, wheelchair to borrow, companion of disabled person free admission. Visitor Centre open 30 March - 7 November.

Admission to Gardens £3.40 Children/concessions £2.20

Gardens OPEN ALL YEAR.

Donation to Scotland's Gardens Scheme

COILTIE, Divach, Drumnadrochit   ♿

(Gillian & David Nelson)

A wooded garden, an amalgamation of a Victorian flower garden abandoned 60 years ago and a walled field with a large moraine, which has been made over the past 15 years. Development work still in progress. Many trees, old and new, mixed shrub and herbaceous borders, roses, wall beds, rockery. No dogs please. Off A82 at Drumnadrochit. Take road signposted Divach uphill 2 miles. Past Divach Lodge, 150m. Admission £1.50 Children free

OPEN DAILY 16th MAY — 31st JULY 12 - 7pm

40% to Amnesty International

DUNVEGAN CASTLE, Isle of Skye

Dating from the 13th century and continuously inhabited by the Chiefs of MacLeod, this romantic fortress stronghold occupies a magnificent lochside setting. The gardens, originally laid out in the 18th century, have been extensively replanted and include lochside walks, woodlands and water gardens. Licensed restaurant. Two craft shops. clan exhibition. Seal colony. Loch boat trips. Admission to Castle and Garden inclusive £5, students, OAPs & parties £4.50, children £2.50. Dunvegan village 1mile, 23 miles west of Portree.

Admission to gardens: £3.50 Children £2.00

Castle & gardens November to March 11am – 4pm. Last entry 3.30pm

Monday 23rd MARCH to Saturday 31st OCTOBER 10am - 5.30pm. Last entry 5pm

Donation to Scotland's Gardens Scheme

GLAMAIG, Braes, Portree, Isle of Skye

(Mr & Mrs R Townsend)

Two acres of mixed wild and informal garden with burn, waterfalls and extensive views of sea, islands and mountains. Large collection of unusual shrubs, rhododendrons, olearias etc. Primulas, herbaceous and rock garden. Some plants for sale. 7 miles from Portree at end of B883. Admission £1.50 OAPs £1.00

OPEN DAILY EASTER TO MID-SEPTEMBER

Donation to Scotland's Gardens Scheme

The HOUSE of AIGAS and FIELD CENTRE, by Beauly
(Sir John and Lady Lister-Kaye)
Aigas has a woodland walk overlooking the Beauly River with a collection of named
Victorian specimen trees now being restored and extended with a garden of rockeries,
herbaceous borders and shrubberies. Tea in house. Aigas Field Centre facilities are open
to groups by appointment only: 01463 782443. Route: 4½ miles from Beauly on A831
Cannich/Glen Affric road.
Admission from £1.50
SUNDAY 19th JULY 2 – 5.30pm
Donation to Scotland's Gardens Scheme

HOUSE OF GRUINARD, by Laide
(The Hon Mrs Angus Maclay)
Cottage gardening on a grand scale with wonderful west coast views. Herbaceous and
shrub borders and water garden. Large variety of plants for sale. Sorry no teas.
Admission £2.00 Children under 16 free
WEDNESDAYS 3rd & 24th JUNE and 5th AUGUST 2 – 5pm
40% to Highland Hospice

 # The HYDROPONICUM, Achiltibuie   (lower level)
(The Rt Hon Viscount Gough)
Situated further north than Moscow, this unique indoor garden overlooks the beautiful
Summer Isles. Personally guided tours take visitors into the Garden of the Future and
through three different climatic zones. Lush, sub-tropical fruit trees, exotic flowers, herbs
and vegetables all grow without soil. Cascading floral spiral. Hydroponic gift shop and
Lilypond Cafe. Route: turn off A835 on to single track road to Achiltibuie and follow
signs.
Admission £4.00 Children £2.00 Concessions £3.00 Family ticket £10.00
SUNDAYS 19th JULY & 16th AUGUST 10am – 6pm
40% to R N L I

INVEREWE, Poolewe
(The National Trust for Scotland)
Magnificent 50-acre Highland garden, surrounded by mountains, moorland and sea-loch.
Founded in 1862 by Osgood Mackenzie, it now includes Australian tree ferns, exotic
plants from China and a magnificent *magnolia campbellii*. Visitor centre, shop and self-
service restaurant.
Admission £4.80 Children & OAPs £3.20 Family £12.80
SATURDAY 25th APRIL and SUNDAY 26th JULY 9.30 - 9pm
40% to The Gardens Fund of the National Trust for Scotland
For further opening details see page 128

KILCOY CASTLE, Muir of Ord
(Mr & Mrs Nick McAndrew)
16th century castle (not open) surrounded by extensive terraced lawns, walled garden
with fine herbaceous and shrub borders, surrounding vegetable garden. Woodland areas
with rhododendrons, azaleas and particularly fine mature trees and shrubs. Teas. Route:
A9 to Tore roundabout, A832 signed Beauly and Muir of Ord. After 1½ miles, turn right
at church signed Kilcoy, entrance is ½ mile on left.
Admission £1.50 Children 50p
SUNDAY 5th JULY 2 – 6pm
40% to Highland Hospice

KYLLACHY, Tomatin ♿
(The Rt Hon Lord & Lady Macpherson)
Rhododendrons (mainly white), azaleas, meconopsis, primulas, delphiniums, heather beds, herbaceous, alpines, iris. Water garden with stream and ponds. Walled vegetable garden. Plant stall. No dogs please. Cars free. A9 to Tomatin, turn off to Findhorn Bridge, turn west to Coignafearn. Kyllachy House one mile on right.
Admission £1.50   Free car parking.
SUNDAYS 7th JUNE & 26th JULY 2 – 5 pm
40% to The Highland Hospice

LECKMELM SHRUBBERY & ARBORETUM, by Ullapool
(Mr & Mrs Peter Troughton)
The arboretum, planted in the 1870s, is full of splendid and rare trees, specie rhododendrons, azaleas and shrubs. Warmed by the Gulf Stream, this tranquil woodland setting has an alpine garden and paths which lead down to the sea.
Parking in walled garden.Situated by the shore of Loch Broom 3 miles south of Ullapool on the A835 Inverness/Ullapool road.
Admission £1.50 Children under 16 free
OPEN DAILY 1st APRIL to 30th SEPTEMBER 10 am – 6 pm
20% to The Highland Hospice 20% to Scotland's Gardens Scheme

LOCHALSH WOODLAND GARDEN, Balmacara
(The National Trust for Scotland)
This 13-acre policy woodland enoys a tranquil setting by the shore of Loch Alsh. Unique collections of hardy ferns, fuchsias, hydrangeas, bamboos and rhododendrons. New additions include plants from New Zealand and Tasmania. Signposted off A87, 3miles east of Kyle of Lochalsh.
Admission £1.00 Children 50p
SATURDAY 20th JUNE 1 – 5 pm
40% to The Gardens Fund of The National Trust for Scotland
For other opening details see page 128

SEA VIEW GARDEN, Durnamuck, Dundonnell ♿
(Simone & Ian Nelson)
Small, ½ acre cottage garden spectacularly positioned on the side of Little Loch Broom. The flourishing result of one woman's ongoing contest with virgin moor and the elements. Regret no dogs. Limited parking. Plant stall. Refreshments available at the Dundonnell Hotel, 6 miles away. One mile off main A832 Gairloch/Dundonnell road at Badcaul. Turn right 400m after Dundonnell Post Office.
Admission £1.00 Children free with adults
MAY — SEPTEMBER or by appointment. Tel: 01854 633317
20% to Dundonnell Area Community Events   20% to Cancer Relief Macmillan Fund

---

TOURNAIG, Poolewe ♿ (partly)
(Lady Horlick)
Woodland, herbaceous and water garden. Plant stall. Tea in house. 1½ miles north of Inverewe Garden, Poolewe, on main road. Can be viewed at any time, tel: 01445 781250 or 339.
Admission £1.50 Children under 12 free
WEDNESDAYS 27th MAY and 12th AUGUST 2pm
20% to St John's Ambulance   20% to Poolewe Swimming Pool

ROXBURGH

District Organiser:	**Mrs M D Blacklock,** Stable House, Maxton, St Boswells TD6 0EX
Area Organisers:	**The Hon Moyra Campbell,** Scraesburgh, Jedburgh TD8 6QR
Hon. Treasurer:	**Mr J Mackie,** Bank of Scotland, Newton St Boswells TD6 0PG

DATES OF OPENING

Floors Castle, Kelso	Daily Easter to end October	10am – 4.30pm
Newton Don Policies, Kelso	Sunday 17 May	11.30 – 5pm
Corbet Tower, Morebattle	Sunday 12 July	2 – 6pm
Monteviot, Jedburgh	Sunday 19 July	2 – 5pm
Yetholm Village Gardens	Sunday 2 August	2 – 6pm
St Boswells Village Gardens	Sunday 9 August	2 – 6pm

CORBET TOWER, Morebattle
(Mr & Mrs G H Waddell)
Scottish baronial house (1896) set in parkland in the foothills of the Cheviots. Garden includes formal parterre with old fashioned roses. Traditional walled garden with herbaceous borders, herbs and vegetables. Woodland and water garden. Teas. Plant and vegetable stall. From A68 Jedburgh road take A698, at Eckford B6401 to Morebattle, then road marked Hownam. Dogs on lead please.
Admission £2.00 Children under 14 free
SUNDAY 12th JULY 2 - 6pm
40% to Marie Curie Cancer Care (Borders branch)

FLOORS CASTLE, Kelso &
(The Duke of Roxburghe)
Floors Castle is situated in beautiful Borders country, overlooking Kelso and the River Tweed. Extensive gardens, grounds and children's play area. Ample parking facilities. Garden Centre & Coffee Shop open daily 10.30 am - 5.30 pm; also Castle, grounds & restaurant. (Last admission to House 4 pm). Nearest town Kelso.
Open Daily EASTER to end OCTOBER 10am - 4.30pm
Donation to Scotland's Gardens Scheme

MONTEVIOT, Jedburgh ♿ (partially)
Monteviot stands on a rise above the River Teviot overlooking the rolling Borders
countryside. Features include a walled rose garden, shrub and herbaceous borders,
water garden of islands linked by bridges, collection of rare trees in pinery.
Rose Day: Royal British Legion Pipe Band. Children's activities. Cream teas in house.
Stalls including cakes, plants and bottle tombola. Car park free. Dogs on lead. St
Boswells 5 miles, Jedburgh 4 miles. Turn off A68 3 miles north of Jedburgh on to B6400.
Entrance second turning on right.
Enquiries to (01835) 830380 9.30am-1pm Monday-Friday.
Admission £2.00 OAPs £1.00 Children under 14 free
SUNDAY 19th JULY (ROSE DAY) 2 - 5 pm
20% to St Mary's Church, Jedburgh
20% to Riding for the Disabled Association, Border Group

NEWTON DON POLICIES, Kelso
(Mr & Mrs William Balfour)
The mansion-house at Newton Don is a Grade A listed Greek Revival building, and its
policies and walks form part of a landscape designed (it is believed) in the 1760s, to make
the most of its fine position on rising ground with views over the Tweed valley to the
Cheviots, and the river Eden which winds its way through woods and parkland to the
north and south. The policies are being slowly reclaimed and restored, and provide
lovely views and walks, an opportunity to explore and be surprised, and an insight into
what 'gardening' on a large scale entails. Why not come early, and bring the children, the
dog (on a lead, please) and a picnic to enjoy on the lawns around the house, or amongst
the bluebells. Weather permitting, there will be some big kites flying from the Orchard
Bank – do bring yours too – and there will be hot soup, tea and shortbread in the house,
whatever the weather. Signposted from the A6089, 3 miles north of Kelso.
Admission £2.00 Children free
SUNDAY 17th MAY 11.30pm – 5pm
40% to Save the Children Fund

 # ST BOSWELLS VILLAGE GARDENS ♿ (some)
An opportunity to see a diversity of 'secret' gardens hidden behind the street facade of St
Boswells. Each has an individual style and approach to gardening, ranging from a
delightful small Georgian house (1765) with an interesting collection of fruit trees, to a
contemporary sculpture garden. A small Arts & Crafts lodge house (1907) offers an
eclectic mix of cottage garden and more unusual plants. Year round colour and interest
combined with low maintenance can be seen in another garden.
Teas. Plant and produce stall.
Parking: on St Boswells village green <u>only</u>, where tickets will be available.
Admission £2.00 includes all open gardens Children free
SUNDAY 9th AUGUST 2 – 6pm
40% to Arthritis Care (Galashiels branch)

YETHOLM VILLAGE GARDENS

Hill View (Mr & Mrs Dodds) **Ivy House** ♿ (Mr & Mrs Patterson)
2 Grafton Court ♿ (Mr G Lee) **Innisfree** ♿ (Mr & Mrs Archer)
5 Yewtree Lane (Mr & Mrs P Boyd) **Bowmont Lodge** (Mr & Mrs Elberson)
Copsewood (Mr & Mrs Fraser Nimmo) **4 Morebattle Road** (Mr & Mrs D White)
3 Morebattle Road (Mr & Mrs D Hutchinson)

Yetholm Village is situated at the foot of the Cheviot Hills with outstanding views. Each garden has its own endearing character and is filled with a variety of herbaceous shrubs, fruit trees and colourful bedding plants. Tickets will be sold on the Village Green where there will be a produce stall. Home baked teas. Ample parking.
Admission £1.50, includes all gardens.
SUNDAY 2nd AUGUST 2 - 6pm
40% to Children's Hospice Association Scotland

STEWARTRY OF KIRKCUDBRIGHT

District Organiser: **Mrs M R C Gillespie,** Danevale Park, Crossmichael, Castle Douglas DG7 2LP

Area Organisers: **Miss P Bain,** Annick Bank, Hardgate, Castle Douglas DG7 3LD

Mrs C Cathcart, Culraven, Borgue, Kirkcudbright DG6 4SG

Mrs A Chandler, Auchenvin, Rockcliffe, Dumfries DG5 4QQ

Mrs Jane Hannay, Kirklandhill, Kirkpatrick Durham, Castle Douglas DG7 3EZ

Mrs J F Mayne, Hazlefield House, Auchencairn, Castle Douglas

Mrs W J McCulloch, Ardwall, Gatehouse of Fleet DG7 2EN

Mrs C A Ramsay, Limits, St Johns, Dalry, Castle Douglas DG7 3SW

Hon. Treasurer: **Mr W Little,** 54 St Andrew Street, Castle Douglas DG7 1EN

DATES OF OPENING

Barnhourie Mill, Colvend .... By appointment
Corsock House, Castle Douglas .... By appointment

Danevale Park, Crossmichael .... Sunday 1 March   2 - 5pm
Walton Park, Castle Douglas................................. Sunday 3 May   2 – 5pm
Barnhourie Mill, Colvend .... Sunday 24 May   2 – 5pm

109

Corsock House, Castle Douglas .... Sunday 31 May		2 – 5pm
Hensol, Mossdale .... Sunday 14 June		2 – 5pm
Cally Gardens, Gatehouse of Fleet .... Sunday 21 June		10am – 5.30pm
Southwick House, Dumfries .... Sunday 28 June		2 – 5pm
	& afternoons 29 June – 3 July	
Argrennan House, Castle Douglas .... Sunday 12 July		2 – 5pm
Threave Garden .... Sunday 2 August		9am-5.30pm
Cally Gardens, Gatehouse of Fleet .... Sunday 9 August		10am – 5.30pm
Arndarroch Cottage, St John's Town of Dalry ...... Sunday 16 August		2 – 5pm
Crofts, Kirkpatrick Durham .... Sunday 23 August		2 - 5pm

---

ARGRENNAN HOUSE, Castle Douglas &

(Robert Reddaway & Tulane Kidd)
Georgian house set in beautiful parkland with specimen trees. A large walled garden with traditional herbaceous borders, shrub borders and rose garden. Water garden with box parterres and 1840 rockery. Water garden, ponds and bog gardens. Plant stall by NCCPG. Teas served in old kitchen. House not open. Route: Castle Douglas 3½ miles. Kirkcudbright 3½ miles on A711.
Admission £2.00 Children 50p
SUNDAY 12th JULY 2 - 5 pm
40% to Crossroads Care Attendant Scheme (Stewartry branch)

ARNDARROCH COTTAGE, St John's Town of Dalry & (partly)

(Anniki and Matt Lindsay)
A young garden created since 1991 on a windswept hillside overlooking Kendoon Loch. Mainly native trees, species and some Old English roses. Herbaceous plants. Small pond and bog garden, kitchen garden and some fruit trees on a 2¼ acre site. The aim is to create a semi-natural environment which is wildlife friendly. Teas at nearby Kendoon Youth Hostel. Plant stall. Dogs on leads please. About 5 miles from St John's Town of Dalry or from Carsphairn on the B700. Parking at Kendoon Youth Hostel. Lifts arranged from here or you may enjoy the 1km walk. Some parking at Arndarroch Cottage for disabled visitors.
Admission £1.50 Children £1.00
SUNDAY 16th AUGUST 2 – 5pm
40% to N C D L, Glencaple Kennels

BARNHOURIE MILL, Colvend & (partly)

(Dr M R Paton)
Flowering shrubs and trees, dwarf conifers and an especially fine collection of rhododendron species. Tea in house £1. Cars free. Dalbeattie 5 miles. Route A710 from Dumfries.
Admission £2.00 Children free
SUNDAY 24th MAY 2 – 5pm
Also open by appointment. Tel: 01387 780269
40% to Scottish Wildlife Trust

CALLY GARDENS, Gatehouse of Fleet ♿
(Mr Michael Wickenden)
A specialist nursery in a fine 2.7 acre, 18th century walled garden with old vinery and
bothy, all surrounded by the Cally Oak woods. Our collection of 3,500 varieties can be
seen and a selection will be available pot-grown, especially rare herbaceous perennials.
Forestry nature trails nearby. Route: From Dumfries take the Gatehouse turning off A75
and turn left, through the Cally Palace Hotel Gateway from where the gardens are well
signposted. Admission charge: £1.50. Open 11th April–25th October: Tues–Frid
2–5.30pm, Sat & Sun 10am–5.30pm. Closed Mondays.
SUNDAYS 21st JUNE & 9th AUGUST 10am – 5.30pm
40% to Save the Children Fund

CORSOCK HOUSE, Castle Douglas
(Mr & Mrs M L Ingall)
Rhododendrons, woodland walks with temples , water gardens and loch. David Bryce
turretted "Scottish Baronial" house in background. Teas by Corsock WRI. Cars free.
Dumfries 14 miles, Castle Douglas 10 miles, Corsock ½ mile on A712.
Admission £2.00 Children 50p
SUNDAY 31st MAY 2 - 5 pm
Also open by appointment: Tel. 01644 440250
40% to Gardeners' Royal Benevolent Society

 # CROFTS, Kirkpatrick Durham ♿ **(partly)**
(Mr & Mrs Andrew Dalton)
Victorian garden and policies in the process of renovation and extension. Teas.
A75 to Crocketford, then 3 miles on A711. Admission £2.00. Children 50p.
SUNDAY 23rd AUGUST 2 - 5pm *40% to Corsock & Kirkpatrick Durham Church*

DANEVALE PARK, Crossmichael
(Mrs M R C Gillespie)
Open for snowdrops. Woodland walks. Tea in house. Route: A713. Crossmichael 1 mile,
Castle Douglas 3 miles. Admission £1.50
SUNDAY 1st MARCH 2 - 5pm *40% to Crossmichael Village Hall*

HENSOL, Mossdale, Castle Douglas ♿
(Lady Henderson)
An early 19th century granite house designed by Lugar. Established garden surrounding
house. Alpines, shrubs, water garden and new woodland garden. River walks. Plant
stall. Cars free. Tea in house. Route: A762, 3 miles north of Laurieston.
Admission £2.00 Children 50p
SUNDAY 14th JUNE 2 - 5 pm *40% to R N L I*

SOUTHWICK HOUSE, Dumfries ♿
(Mrs C H Thomas)
Formal garden with lily ponds and herbaceous borders, shrubs, vegetables, fruit and
greenhouse. Water garden with boating pond, lawns and fine trees, through which flows
the Southwick burn. Cream teas, ice cream and soft drinks. On A710, near Caulkerbush.
Dalbeattie 7 miles, Dumfries 17 miles.
Admission £2.00 Children 50p
SUNDAY 28th JUNE 2 - 5 pm also Monday 29th June–Friday 3rd July. Honesty box
40% to Childline Scotland

111

THREAVE GARDEN, Castle Douglas &

(The National Trust for Scotland)

Home of the Trust's School of Practical Gardening. Spectacular daffodils in spring, colourful herbaceous borders in summer, striking autumn trees and heather garden. Plant stall. Route: A75, one mile west of Castle Douglas.

Admission £4.00 Children & OAPs £2.70 Family £10.70

SUNDAY 2nd AUGUST 9.30am – 5.30pm

40% to The Gardens Fund of The National Trust for Scotland

For other opening details see page 132

WALTON PARK, Castle Douglas &

(Mr Jeremy Brown)

Walled garden, gentian border. Flowering shrubs, rhododendrons and azaleas. Cars free. Tea in house. Plant stall. Route: B794, 3½ miles from A75.

Admission £2.00

SUNDAY 3rd MAY 2 - 5 pm

40% to Carnsalloch Cheshire Home

STIRLING

District Organiser:	**Lady Edmonstone,** Duntreath Castle, Blanefield G63 9AJ
Area Organisers:	**Mrs John Carr,** Duchray Castle, Aberfoyle FK8 3XL
	Mrs Guy Crawford, St Blanes House, Dunblane FK15 0ER
	Mrs Robin Hunt, Keirhill, Balfron G83 0LG
	Mrs John Stein, Southwood, Southfield Crescent, Stirling FK8 2QJ
	Mrs Patrick Stirling-Aird, Old Kippenross, Dunblane FK15 0CQ
	The Hon Mrs R E G Younger, Old Leckie, Gargunnock FK8 3BN
Hon. Treasurer:	**Mr A Kingsley,** Royal Bank of Scotland, 82 Murray Place, Stirling FK8 2DR

DATES OF OPENING

Daldrishaig House, Aberfoyle .... May to July, by appointment

Kilbryde Castle, Dunblane .... All year, by appointment

Kilbryde Castle, Dunblane	Sunday 19 April	2 – 5pm
Kilbryde Castle, Dunblane	Sunday 10 May	2 – 5pm
The Pass House, Kilmahog	Sunday 17 May	2 – 5pm
Orchardlea House, Callander	Sunday 24 May	2 – 5pm

Shrubhill, Hill of Row	Sunday 31 May	2 – 5pm
Blairuskin Lodge, Kinlochard	Wednesday 3 June	2 – 5pm
Duntreath Castle, Blanefield	Sunday 7 June	2 – 5pm
Kilbryde Castle, Dunblane	Sunday 7 June	2 – 5pm
Lochdochart, Crianlarich	Sunday 7 June	12 – 5pm
Daldrishaig House and		
The Practice Garden, Aberfoyle	Wednesday 10 June	2 – 5pm
Ballindalloch, Balfron	Sunday 14 June	2–5.30pm
Dunblane Town Gardens	Sunday 21 June	2 – 5pm
Kilbryde Castle, Dunblane	Sunday 5 July	2 – 5pm
Callander Lodge, Callander	Sunday 12 July	2 – 5pm
Kilbryde Castle, Dunblane	Sunday 9 August	2 – 5pm
The Walled Garden, E Lodge, Gean	Sunday 16 August	2 – 5pm
Thorntree, Arnprior	Sunday 23 August	2 – 5pm
Kilbryde Castle, Dunblane	Sunday 6 September	2 – 5pm
SGS Autumn Lecture, Stirling	Thursday 1 October	10.30am–4pm

BALLINDALLOCH, Balfron　&

(Mr & Mrs A M M Stephen)
On the site of an earlier castle, a Victorian country house was dramatically reduced
around 1980 and the gardens re-planned for present day maintenance. Small
Ballindalloch exhibition (free). Paved terraces and ruin garden with 17th century obelisk
sundial. Shrubs and perennials include recent planting amid lawns and woodland with
views of the Campsie Fells. Teas by Balfron WRI. Plant stall. Route: A875 between
Killearn and Balfron.
Admission £2.00 Children under 12 free
SUNDAY 14th JUNE 2 – 5.30pm
40% to R N L I (Strathendrick)

BLAIRUSKIN LODGE, Kinlochard

(Mr & Mrs D Miller)
Flowering shrubs, rhododendrons, woodland walk, vegetable garden, small cottage
garden. Restricted parking. Teas. Plant stall. Route: A81 Glasgow to Aberfoyle. 6 miles
from Aberfoyle on Inversnaid Road, one mile from Forest Hills.
Admission £1.50 Children under 12 free
WEDNESDAY 3rd JUNE 2 – 5pm
40% to Matthew Miller Cancer Fund

CALLANDER LODGE, Leny Feus, Callander

(Miss Caroline Penney)
Romantic Victorian garden. Three acres of mature trees, specimen shrubs, lawns and
herbaceous borders. Waterfall pool and fern grotto. Bog garden. Harmony walk.
Vegetable garden. Tea and biscuits. Plant stall. Route: A84 west through Callander,
turn right at sign for Leny Feus. Garden is at end on left.
Admission £2.00
SUNDAY 12th JULY 2 – 5pm
40% to Camphill, Blair Drummond

DALDRISHAIG HOUSE, Aberfoyle
(Mr & Mrs John J Blanche)
2½ acre plantsman's garden. Water, scree and herbaceous gardens. Home made teas in the conservatory. Plant stall. Continue straight through Aberfoyle towards Kinlochard for 1½ miles. Very restricted parking. Free minibus service from Aberfoyle car park, taking in The Practice Garden in village.
JOINT OPENING WITH THE PRACTICE GARDEN as featured on BBC TV's 'Beechgrove Garden'
Admission £1.50 Children free
WEDNESDAY 10th JUNE 2 - 5 pm
Small and large private parties welcome by appointment May to July. Tel: 01877 382223
40% to Crossroads Care Attendant Scheme

DUNBLANE TOWN GARDENS &. (some)
A good selection of interesting town gardens, both large and small, providing a great variety of plants. Plant stalls. Tea shops in Dunblane. Entrance badge and map with garden descriptions available from any open garden. These will be well signposted.
Route: B8033 off A9, six miles north of Stirling.
Admission £2.00 Children free OAPs £1.00
SUNDAY 21st JUNE 2 – 5pm
40% to Strathcarron Hospice

DUNTREATH CASTLE, Blanefield &.
(Sir Archibald Edmonstone)
Extensive gardens with mature and new plantings. Landscaped lake, water and bog gardens. Formal garden, rhododendrons and woodland walk. 15th century keep and chapel. Pipe band and dancing display. Plant, home cooking and bric-a-brac stalls. Home made teas. Route: A81 north of Glasgow between Blanefield and Killearn.
Admission £2.00 Children free
SUNDAY 7th JUNE 2 – 5pm
40% between Leonard Cheshire Foundation and St Mary's, Aberfoyle

---

KILBRYDE CASTLE, Dunblane, Perthshire &. (partly)
(Lady Campbell & Jack Fletcher)
Traditional Scottish baronial house rebuilt 1877 to replace building dating from 1461.

Partly mature gardens with additions and renovations since 1970. Lawns overlooking Ardoch Burn with wood and water garden still to be completed. Three miles from Dunblane and Doune, signposted from both. No teas. No dogs. Children to be controlled. No toilets. Plants usually for sale.
Admission £2.00 Children under 16 and OAPs £1.50
SUNDAYS 19th APRIL, 10th MAY, 7th JUNE, 5th JULY, 9th AUGUST, 6th SEPTEMBER 2 - 5pm.
40% to Leighton Library, Strathcarron Hospice, Cancer Relief Macmillan Fund and the Friends of Dunblane Cathedral
Also by appointment: 01786 823104

LOCHDOCHART, Crianlarich ♿
(Seona & John Christie of Lochdochart)
Walled garden – fruit, flowers and vegetables. Mature policy woods - rhododendrons and azaleas. Picnic beach by Loch Iubhair. Home made teas. Plant and produce stall. Canoe hire and instruction. Bring your picnic lunch. No dogs please. Route: A85, 4 miles west of Crianlarich. Stone pillars on north side of road.
Admission £1.00 Children free
SUNDAY 7th JUNE 12 - 4pm
40% to Crianlarich Hall

ORCHARDLEA HOUSE., Callander ♿
(Hilary and Rod Gunkel)
"Secret" garden of about half an acre with a wide variety of trees, shrubs and flowers, open this year in late spring. Plant stall. Teas on the terrace. Sorry no dogs. Disabled parking only. At east end of Callander main street (A84). 5 mins. walk from centre of town.
Admission £1.00 Children under 14 free
SUNDAY 24th MAY 2 - 5pm
40% to Chest, Heart & Stroke Scotland

THE PASS HOUSE, Kilmahog, Callander ♿ (partly)
(Dr & Mrs D Carfrae)
Well planted medium sized garden with steep banks down to swift river. Camellias, rhododendrons, azaleas, alpines and shrubs. Propagating house. Teas. Plant stall. 2 miles from Callander on A84 to Lochearnhead.
Admission £1.00 Children free
SUNDAYS 17th MAY 2 - 5 pm
40% to Crossroads Care Attendant Scheme

 # THE PRACTICE GARDEN, Aberfoyle
(The Medical Centre)
A small but unique community garden surrounding the local doctors' surgery. Interesting plants and herbs, a magnificent sequoia and low allergen garden, with original sculptures by local artists. No parking.
Admission £1.00 Children free
Free minibus service from Aberfoyle car park, taking in Daldrishaig on Loch Ard.
JOINT OPENING WITH DALDRISHAIG as featured on BBC TV's 'Beechgrove Garden'.
Admission £1.00 Children free
WEDNESDAY 10th JUNE 2 - 5 pm
40% to Crossroads Care Attendant Scheme

 # SHRUBHILL, Hill of Row ♿
(Martin & Sue Garrett-Cox)
This garden was started 25 years ago and includes shrubs, primulas, rock garden and pond. Teas. Plant Stall. At exit 11 of M9, one mile south of Dunblane, take B824 signed to Doune for exactly two miles. Shrubhill drive on left.
Admission £2.00 Children free
SUNDAY 31st MAY 2 – 5pm
40% to Save the Children Fund

THORNTREE, Arnprior   ♿
(Mark & Carol Seymour)
Courtyard with flower beds all around. Small cottage garden created five years ago.
Fern garden and small woodland underplanted with shade loving plants. Working dried
flower area will be in full production in August. Cream teas. Plant stall. Cake stall. No
dogs please. Route: A811. In Arnprior take Fintry Road, Thorntree is second on right.
Admission £1.50 Children over 12 50p
SUNDAY 23rd AUGUST 2 - 5pm
40% Fintry Driving Group RDA

THE WALLED GARDEN, East Lodge, Gean House, Alloa   ♿
(Mr & Mrs A Scott)
One acre Victorian walled garden with original espaliered walks and central arbour.
Mixed herbaceous borders. Large greenhouses. Recreated as faithfully as possible over
the last five years. Woodland walk with decorative implements. Teas.
Take Stirling /Tullibody road straight through Tullibody. Second entrance on right after
Jaegar factory.
Admission £1.00
SUNDAY 16th AUGUST 2 - 5pm
40% to Enable

SGS AUTUMN LECTURE & BUFFET LUNCH
The Albert Hall, Stirling
"Garden Design – Planning and Planting" by Rosemary Alexander FRSA.
THURSDAY 1st OCTOBER 10.30am – 4pm Full details on page 153

> "Gardens of England & Wales 1998" published by
> The National Gardens Scheme of England & Wales
> is available from
> NGS, Hatchlands Park, East Clandon, Guildford GU4 7RT
> at £4.50 or £5.75 including postage

TWEEDDALE

District Organiser:	**Mrs John Kennedy,** Hazlieburn, West Linton EH46 7AS
Area Organisers:	**Mrs D Balfour-Scott,** Langlawhill, Broughton, Lanarkshire ML12 6HL
	Mrs R K Brown, Runic Cross, Waverley Road, Innerleithen EH44 6QH
	Mrs H B Marshall, Baddinsgill, West Linton, EH46 7HL
Hon. Treasurer:	**Mr K St C Cunningham,** Hallmanor, Peebles EH45 9JN

DATES OF OPENING

Glenhighton, Broughton .... Last Thursday June–September 12.30–5pm
Kailzie Gardens, Peebles .... Daily 21 March – 17 October   11 – 5.30pm
Winter daylight hours, gardens only

Dawyck Botanic Garden	Sunday 10 May	9.30am – 6pm
Haystoun, Peebles	Sunday 24 May	2 – 5.30pm
Hallmanor, Kirkton Manor	Sunday 7 June	2 – 6pm
Stobo Water Garden, Stobo	Sunday 14 June	2 – 6pm
Portmore, Eddleston	Sunday 26 July	2 – 5pm
West Linton Village Gardens	Sunday 9 August	2 - 6pm

DAWYCK BOTANIC GARDEN, Stobo ♿ (limited access)
(Specialist Garden of the Royal Botanic Garden, Edinburgh)
Arboretum of rare trees, rhododendrons and other shrubs. Terraces and stonework
constructed by Italian landscape gardeners in 1820. Conservatory shop with plant sales,
coffees and teas. Guide dogs only. Route: 8 miles south west of Peebles on B712.
Admission £3.00 Concessions £2.50 Children £1.00p Families £7.00
SUNDAY 10th MAY 9.30am – 6pm
40% to Royal Botanic Garden, Edinburgh
For other opening details see page

GLENHIGHTON, Broughton ♿ (partially)
(Iris & Michael Strachan)
5 acres in magnificent surroundings at 750 ft. dating from the early 1970s. Intersected by
Cardon Burn. National Collection of Rosa Pimpinellifolia (Scots briar) being increased
and identified, also of Symphytum (comfrey) in process of being handed on. Spring,
autumn and cottage gardens, pool, lake, woodland walk, rare trees & plants. Light
lunches & teas available at Laurel Bank Tea Room in Broughton, or you may picnic in the
garden. Plant stall. Dogs on leads only. Off A701, turn SW at sign for Glenholm, south
of Broughton. 2½ miles up Glenholm, signed Glenhighton.
Admission £1.50   Well behaved children free
THURSDAYS 12.30 – 5pm: 25th JUNE (Roses) **30th JULY, 27th AUGUST and
24th SEPTEMBER** (Autumn colour)
40% to The National Trust for Scotland (Newhailes Appeal)

HALLMANOR, Kirkton Manor, Peebles
(Mr K St C Cunningham)
Rhododendrons and azaleas, primulas, wooded grounds with loch and salmon ladder.
Set in one of the most beautiful valleys in the Borders. Teas. Plant stall. Peebles 6 miles.
Off A72 Peebles/Glasgow road. Follow SGS signs.
Admission £1.50 Children free
SUNDAY 7th JUNE 2 - 6 pm
40% to Manor & Lyne Churches

HAYSTOUN, Peebles ♿ (partly)
(Mr & Mrs D Coltman)
16th century house (not open). Walled garden, recently planted wild garden with newly created ornamental loch which has beautiful walks around it. Teas. Plant stall. Dogs on lead only please. A703 Edinburgh/Peebles over Tweed bridge in Peebles, follow SGS signs for 1½ miles.
Admission £1.50 Children free
SUNDAY 24th MAY 2 - 5.30pm
40% to The Leonard Cheshire Foundation in Scotland

KAILZIE GARDENS, Peebles ♿
(Lady Buchan-Hepburn)
Semi-formal walled garden with rose garden, herbaceous borders and old fashioned roses. Greenhouses. Woodland and burnside walks among massed spring bulbs and, later, rhododendrons and azaleas. The gardens, set among fine old trees, lie in the beautiful Tweed valley with views across to the Border hills. Free car park. Picnic area. Children's play corner. Home made teas and lunches in licensed restaurant. Art Gallery. Shop. Plant stalls. Stocked trout pond. Parties by arrangement.
Admission: Summer £2.00, children 5-14 50p Winter £1.00, children 50p
OPEN ALL YEAR ROUND Summer: 21st March - 17th October 11am - 5.30pm.
Winter: during daylight hours, the gardens only.
Special Snowdrop Days as advertised locally.
Donation to Scotland's Gardens Scheme

PORTMORE, Eddleston
(Mr & Mrs D H L Reid)
Herbaceous borders. Herb garden. Ornamental vegetable garden. Greenhouse with Victorian grotto. Shrub rose garden and parterre. Cream teas. Dogs on lead please. Edinburgh to Peebles bus No.62.
Admission £2.00
SUNDAY 26th JULY 2 - 5 pm
40% to Crossroads Care Attendant Scheme

STOBO WATER GARDEN, Stobo, Peebles
(Mr Hugh Seymour & Mr Charles Seymour)
Water garden, lakes, azaleas and rhododendrons. Woodland walks. Cars free. Cream teas in village hall. Peebles 7 miles, signposted on B712 Lyne/Broughton road.
Admission £1.50 Children free
SUNDAY 14th JUNE 2 - 6 pm
20% to Stobo Kirk, 20% to The Leonard Cheshire Foundation in Scotland

WEST LINTON VILLAGE GARDENS ♿ (partially)
A number of gardens, small and large, varying from an extensive selection of original stone troughs, to a well established plantsman's garden. Also traditional summer bedding and a small walled garden. Route: A701 or A702 and follow signs. Tickets and maps available at car park or Graham Institute (Teas and Plant Stall) in centre of village.
Admission £2.00 includes all gardens. Children free
SUNDAY 9th AUGUST 2 - 6pm
20% to Crossroads Care Attendant Scheme   20% to Earl Haig Fund

WIGTOWN

District Organiser: **Mrs Francis Brewis,** Ardwell House, Stranraer DG9 9LY

Area Organisers: **Mrs V WolseleyBrinton,** Chlenry, Castle Kennedy,
     Stranraer DG9 8SL
     Mrs Andrew Gladstone, Craichlaw, Kirkcowan,
     Newton Stewart DG8 0DQ

Hon. Treasurer: **Mr G S Fleming,** Bank of Scotland, 64 George Street,
     Stranraer DG9 7JN

DATES OF OPENING

Ardwell House Gardens, Ardwell .... Daily 1st April – 30 September   10am–5pm

Castle Kennedy & Lochinch Gardens,
   Stranraer .... Daily 1st April – 30 September   10am-5pm

Whitehills, Newton Stewart .... 1 April – 31 October by appointment

Logan, Port Logan .... Sunday 24 May   10am – 6pm
Logan Botanic Garden, Port Logan .... Sunday 24 May   10am – 6pm
Whitehills Garden & Nursery, Newton Stewart ... Sunday 7 June   2 – 5pm
Monreith House Garden, Port William .... Sunday 28 June   10am – 5pm
Craichlaw, Kirkcowan .... Sunday 26 July   2 – 5pm

ARDWELL HOUSE GARDENS, Ardwell, Stranraer
(Mrs Faith Brewis & Mr Francis Brewis)
Daffodils, spring flowers, rhododendrons, flowering shrubs, coloured foliage and rock
plants. Moist garden at smaller pond and a walk round larger ponds, with views over
Luce Bay. Plants for sale and self-pick fruit in season. Collecting box. House not open.
Dogs welcome on leads. Picnic site on shore. Teas available in Ardwell village. Stranraer
10 miles. Route A76 towards Mull of Galloway.
Admission £1.50 Children & OAPs 50p
DAILY 1st APRIL – 30th SEPTEMBER 10 am – 5 pm
Donation to Scotland's Gardens Scheme

CASTLE KENNEDY & LOCHINCH GARDENS, Stranraer ♿
(The Earl & Countess of Stair)
The gardens are laid out on a peninsula betwen two lochs and extend to 75 acres from the
ruined Castle Kennedy to Lochinch Castle. They are world famous for rhododendrons,
azaleas, magnolias and embothriums and contain specimens from Hooker and other
expeditions. Choice of peaceful walks. Plant centre. Gift shop with refreshments.
Admission charged. 20% discount for parties over 30 people. Cars and disabled free.
Stranraer 5 miles on A75. For further information telephone 01776-702024.
DAILY 1st APRIL – 30th SEPTEMBER 10 am – 5 pm
Donation to Scotland's Gardens Scheme

#CRAICHLAW, Kirkcowan ♿

(Mr & Mrs Andrew Gladstone)
Formal garden around the house, with herbaceous borders. Set in extensive grounds with lawns, lochs and woodland. A path around the main loch leads to a water garden returning past an orchard of old Scottish apple varieties. Teas. Plant stall. Signposted off A75, 8 miles west of Newton Stewart and B733, one mile west of Kirkcowan.
Admission £2.00 Accompanied children under 14 free
SUNDAY 26th JULY 2 – 5pm
40% to Kircowan Parish Church

LOGAN, Port Logan, by Stranraer ♿

(Mr & Mrs M Coburn)
Queen Anne house, 1701. Rare exotic tropical plants and shrubs. Fine specie and hybrid rhododendrons. Route: 14 miles south of Stranraer on A716, 2½ miles from Ardwell village. JOINT OPENING WITH LOGAN BOTANIC GARDEN.
Admission £2.00 includes both gardens Concessions £1.50 Children 50p Families £4.50
SUNDAY 24th MAY 10 am – 6 pm
40% to Port Logan Hall Fund

LOGAN BOTANIC GARDEN, Port Logan, by Stranraer ♿

(Specialist Garden of the Royal Botanic Garden Edinburgh)
One of the most exotic gardens in Britain. Magnificent tree ferns and cabbage palms grow within a walled garden together with a rich array of southern hemisphere plants. Licensed Salad Bar and Shop with gifts, crafts and plant sales; open 10am to 6pm. Guide dogs only. Route: 10m south of Stranraer on A716, then 2½ miles from Ardwell village. JOINT OPENING WITH LOGAN.
Admission £2.00 includes both gardens Concessions £1.50 Children 50p Families £4.50
SUNDAY 24th MAY 10 am - 6 pm
40% to Royal Botanic Garden Edinburgh
For other opening details see page

MONREITH HOUSE GARDEN, Port William

(Sir Michael Maxwell Bt)
Once famous garden created by Sir Herbert Maxwell, one of the great pioneers of Scottish gardening. It has been neglected for over 50 years, but restoration began last year and is continuing. Interesting trees and shrubs. Teas. 2m from Port William off B7021 Port William/Whithorn.
Admission £2.00 includes entry to exhibition of paintings by Sir Herbert Maxwell
SUNDAY 28th JUNE 10am – 5pm
40% to Monreith Trust

WHITEHILLS GARDEN & NURSERY, Newton Stewart ♿

(Mr & Mrs C A Weston)
Informal garden set among mature trees. Large collection of unusual trees and flowering shrubs. Rhododendrons and azaleas (many grown from seeds collected by owners in China and Nepal) grow amidst the sheltered woodland. Ample parking. Newton Stewart 1 mile. Wood of Cree road ¼ mile north of Minnigaff Church (signposted to RSPB reserve). Dogs on lead please.
Admission £2.00 Accompanied children under14 free.
SUNDAY 7th JUNE 2 - 5pm
Open by appointment 1 April - 31 October by appointment: 01671 402049
40% to Friends of Newton Stewart Hospital

🛡 The National Trust for Scotland

GARDENS IN TRUST

THE NATIONAL TRUST FOR SCOTLAND is custodian to some of Scotland's finest gardens, from the world-famous Inverewe and Crathes Castle Gardens to the intriguing 'secret' gardens at Inveresk Lodge and Malleny Gardens, both near Edinburgh.

The Trust's vital conservation work is made possible by the thousands of visitors who enjoy its gardens every year and so contribute financially to their upkeep. Trust gardens are open most days of the year, but we also give active support to Scotland's Gardens Scheme by opening our gardens on its behalf on special days.

We invite you to sample a selection of National Trust for Scotland gardens in the following pages. Further details of Trust properties can be found in our annual *Visit Scotland's Best* brochure (free) or our annual handbook (£2.00 incl. post and packing). Free brochures listing facilities for disabled visitors and regional guides to events taking place at our properties (published in spring) are also available. All may be found at properties or ordered from NTS headquarters, 5 Charlotte Square, Edinburgh EH2 4DU; tel (0131) 243 9393.

Harmony Hall opens to visitors

Set around the early nineteenth-century Harmony Hall (not open to visitors), this attractive walled garden is situated near Priorwood Garden, in the centre of Melrose, and has magnificent views of Melrose Abbey and the Eildon Hills. Opening to visitors for the first time in 1998, the garden comprises lawns, herbaceous and mixed borders, vegetable and fruit areas, and a rich display of spring bulbs. *Open: 1 April to 30 September, Mon–Sat 10–5.30, Sun 1.30–5.30. Admission:£1.00 (honesty box)* **Free admission to members of The National Trust for Scotland**

♛ The National Trust for Scotland

Arduaine Garden

Argyll & Bute. On A816, 20 miles south of Oban and 17 miles north of Lochgilphead. Bus: infrequent service passes garden entrance; tel West Coast Motors (01586) 552319

Branklyn Garden

A85, 116 Dundee Road, Perth. Bus: stop 200 yds from garden; tel Stagecoach (01738) 629339. Rail: Perth station 25 mins walk; tel (0345) 484950

THIS OUTSTANDING 20–acre garden is situated on a promontory bounded by Loch Melfort and Asknish Bay on the Sound of Jura, and is climatically favoured by the Gulf Stream. It is nationally renowned for rhododendrons, azaleas and magnolias and also has a series of ponds and watercourses and many beautiful herbaceous perennials flowering throughout the season. Garden accessible to disabled visitors. For more information tel (01852) 200366.

Open all year, daily 9.30—sunset. Admission: adult £2.40, child/concession £1.60, adult party £1.90, child/school party £1 (family £6.40).
Free admission to members of The National Trust for Scotland

PERCHED ABOVE the city of Perth lie 'the finest two acres of private garden in the country'. Famed for its alpines, *Meconopsis* and autumn colour, Branklyn can provide interest throughout the season. Visitors often find inspiration for their own gardens or peace from today's hustle and bustle at this attractive garden, created by the late Mr and Mrs John Renton. For more information tel (01738) 625535.

Open 1 Mar to 31 Oct, daily 9.30–sunset. Admission: adult £2.40, child/concession £1.60, adult party £1.90, child/school party £1 (family £6.40).
Free admission to members of The National Trust for Scotland.

The National Trust for Scotland
Brodick Castle, Garden and Country Park

Isle of Arran. CalMac Ferries from Ardrossan to Brodick (connecting bus to castle, 2 miles) and Claonaig, Kintyre, to Lochranza; tel (01475) 650100.

BRODICK CASTLE and its gardens came into the care of the Trust in 1958 following the death of the Duchess of Montrose, whose home it was. She created a woodland garden, considered one of the finest rhododendron gardens in Europe. Plants from Himalaya, Burma and China flourish in the gentle west coast climate and give a continuous display of colour from January to August. The formal garden is 250 years old and has recently been restored as a Victorian garden. A country park was established in 1980 through an agreement between the then Cunninghame District Council and the Trust. Special nature trail for disabled. Wheelchairs, electric battery car and braille sheets available. For further information tel (01770) 302202.

Open: Castle, 1 Apr to 31 Oct, daily 11.30–5 (last admission 4.30). Reception Centre and shop (dates as castle), 10–5; restaurant 11– 5. Garden and Country Park, all year, daily 9.30–sunset.

Admission: castle and garden, adult £4.80, child/concession £3.20, adult party £3.80, child/school party £1, family £12.80. Garden only, adult £2.40, child/concession £1.60, adult party £1.90, child/school party £1.

Free admission to members of The National Trust for Scotland.

☙ The National Trust for Scotland

Crathes Castle Garden

On A93, 3 miles east of Banchory and 15 miles west of Aberdeen. Bus: from Aberdeen bus station, tel Bluebird Buses (01224) 212266.

Drum Castle Garden

Off A93, 3 miles west of Peterculter, 8 miles east of Banchory and 10 miles west of Aberdeen. Bus: from Aberdeen bus station, tel Bluebird Buses (01224) 212266

THIS HISTORIC CASTLE AND ITS GARDENS are situated near Banchory, in a delightful part of Royal Deeside. Crathes was formerly the home of Sir James and Lady Burnett, whose lifelong interests found expression in the gardens and in one of the best plant collections to be found in Britain. No less than eight colourful gardens can be found within the walled garden. Wheelchair access to gardens and grounds, trail for disabled visitors, toilet with disabled access, shop, exhibitions, adventure playground and restaurant. For further information tel (01330) 844525.

Open: castle, Visitor Centre, shop & licensed restaurant, 1 Apr to 31 Oct, daily 11–5.30 (last admission to castle 4.45); plant sales, same dates except weekends only in Oct. Other times by appointment only. Admission to castle is by timed ticket (limited number available each day: entry may be delayed). Garden & grounds, all year, daily 9.30 – sunset. Grounds may be closed at short notice on very busy days due to the limited capacity for car parking. Admission: castle only, adult £2, child/ concession £1.30, combined ticket (castle, garden & grounds), adult £4.80, child/concession £3.20, adult party £3.80, child/school party £1, family £12.80. Grounds only/walled garden only, adult £2, child/ concession £1.30. Grounds and walled garden, adult £4, child/concession £2.60. **Free admission to members of The National Trust for Scotland**

THE COMBINATION OF a thirteenth-century square tower, a fine Jacobean mansion house and the additions of Victorian lairds make Drum Castle unique among Scottish castles. In the walled garden the Trust has created a unique Garden of Historic Roses, the design of each quadrant representing a different century of gardening, from the seventeenth to the twentieth. The pleasant parkland surroundings contain the 100-acre Old Wood of Drum, coniferous plantations and deciduous woodland, and offer fine views. For further information tel (01330) 811204.

Open: castle, Good Friday to Easter Monday and 1 May to 30 Sep, daily 1.30–5.30; weekends in Oct, 1.30–5.30 (last admission 4.45). Garden, same dates, daily 10–6. Grounds, all year, daily 9.30–sunset.

Admission: castle, garden and grounds £4.20, child/concession £2.80, adult party £3.40, child/ school party £1, family £11.20. Garden and grounds only, adult £2, child/concession £1.30, adult party £1.60, child/school party £1. **Free admission to members of The National Trust for Scotland.**

♛ The National Trust for Scotland
Culzean Castle, Garden and Country Park

South Ayrshire. A719, 4 miles west of Maybole and 12 miles south of Ayr. Bus: hourly service Ayr–Girvan via Maidens passes main entrance; tel (0141) 226 4826

CULZEAN CASTLE AND COUNTRY PARK is the Trust's most visited garden property and one of the major tourist attractions in Scotland. The range of interests and activities at Culzean makes it a perfect day out for the family.

The Fountain Garden lies in front of Robert Adam's magnificent castle, with terraces and herbaceous borders reflecting its Georgian elegance. Scotland's first Country Park, consisting of 563 acres, contains a wealth of interest from shoreline through Deer Park, Swan Pond to mature parklands, gardens, woodland walks and adventure playground. A conservatory has been resored to its former glory as an orangery, and recent restorations include the Ruined Arch, Viaduct, Ice House, a unique Pagoda and the beautiful Camellia House.

Ranger/naturalists located at the Visitor Centre provide excellent services for visitors including many guided walks. An environmental education service and interpretation programme are based on the Country Park.

The Visitor Centre facilities include shops, licensed self-service restaurants, introductory exhibitions, auditorium and information. For disabled visitors there is a lift in the castle, toilets, wheelchairs and induction loop for the hard of hearing.

For further information tel (01655) 760274.

Open: castle, Visitor Centre, licensed restaurant and shops, 1 April to 31 October, daily 10.30 – 5.30 (last admission 5). Other times by appointment. Country Park, all year, daily 9.30 – sunset.

Admission: combined ticket, castle and country park, adult £6.50, child/concession £4.40, adult party £5.50, child/school party £2, family £17. Counry Park only, adult £3.50, child/ concession £2.40, adult party £3, child/school party £1, school coach £20, family £9.

Free admission to members of The National Trust for Scotland.

☙ The National Trust for Scotland

Culross Palace Garden

Fife. Off A985, 12 miles west of Forth Road Bridge and 4 miles east of Kincardine Bridge.
Bus: Fife Scottish, tel (01383) 621249

Falkland Palace Garden

Fife. A912, 11 miles north of Kirkcaldy
Bus: Fife Scottish, tel (01592) 610686

In 1994 the Trust reopened Culross Palace and Garden following three years of restoration. The Palace, built between 1597 and 1611, was not a royal palace but the home of Sir George Bruce, a wealthy merchant and pioneer entrepreneur. A model seventeenth-century garden created by the Trust shows a selection of the plants which might have been available to Sir George Bruce to support the needs of his household. These include a range of vegetables, culinary and medicinal herbs, soft fruit, ornamental shrubs and herbaceous perennials. Terraced and on a steep slope, the garden is laid out in a series of raised beds. Willow hurdle fences, crude rustic plant-supports and crushed-shell paths add to the period effect. For further information tel (01383) 880359.

Open: palace, 1 Apr to 30 Sep, daily 11-5 (last admission 4). Town House & Study, same dates, 1.30–5 and weekends in Oct. 11– 5. Groups at other times by appt. Tearoom (in Bessie Bar Hall), dates as Town House, 10.30 – 4.30. Admission: combined ticket (Palace, Study & Town House), adult £4.20, child/concession £2.80, adult party £3.40, child/school party £1, family £11.20. **Free admission to members of The National Trust for Scotland.**

THE ROYAL PALACE of Falkland, set in the heart of a medieval village, was the country residence and hunting lodge of eight Stuart monarchs, including Mary, Queen of Scots. The palace gardens were restored by the late Keeper, Major Michael Crichton Stuart, to a design by Percy Cane. Trees, shrubs and herbaceous borders give a long-lasting display – from spring-flowering cherries to the rich autumn colouring of the maples. Ramp into garden for wheelchairs.

For further information tel (01337) 857397.

Open: palace & garden, 1 Apr to 31 Oct, Mon–Sat 11–5.30, Sun 1.30–5.30 (last admission to palace 4.30, to garden 5). Groups at other times by appointment. Town Hall, by appointment only.

Admission: palace and garden, adult £4.80, child/concession £3.20, adult party £3.80, child/ school party £1, family £12.80. Garden only, adult £2.40, child/concession £1.60, adult party £1.90, child/school party £1. Scots Guards and members of the Scots Guards Association, wearing the Association's badge, admitted free. **Free admission to members of The National Trust for Scotland.**

♼ The National Trust for Scotland

Hill of Tarvit Garden

Fife. Off A916, 2¹/₂ miles south of Cupar. Bus: Fife Scottish to Ceres (1 mile); tel (01334) 474238

BOTH HOUSE AND GARDEN were remodelled by Sir Robert Lorimer in 1906 and the result is a wonderful mix of formal gardens and parkland. Visitors can wander through the fragrant walled garden with its herbaceous borders, linger on the terraces catching glimpses of the glorious view through ornamental yews, or enjoy the heady rose scent in the sunken garden.

For further information tel (01334) 653127.

Open: house, Good Friday to Easter Monday and 1 May to 30 Sep, daily 1.30–5.30, weekends in Oct, 1.30 – 5.30 (last admission 4.45). Tearoom, same dates, but opens 12.30. Garden & grounds, 1 Apr to 31 Oct, daily 9.30am–9pm; 1 Nov to 31 Mar, daily 9.30–4.30.

Admission: house and garden, adult £3.70, child/concession £2.50, adult party £3, child/school party £1, family £9.90. Garden & grounds only, £1 (honesty box).

Free admission to members of The National Trust for Scotland.

Inveresk Lodge Garden

East Lothian. A6124, near Musselburgh, 6 miles east of Edinburgh. Bus: LRT from Edinburgh, tel (0131) 555 6363

THIS ATTRACTIVE TERRACED garden is located in the historic village of Inveresk, on the outskirts of Edinburgh. Most of the plants hold the Royal Horticultural Society's Award of Garden Merit and highlights include the excellent range of roses and shrubs. The woodland area is especially delightful in autumn. The garden provides the setting for the seventeenth-century Inveresk Lodge (not open to visitors), the oldest house in the village. For further information tel (01721) 722502.

Open: 1 Apr to 30 Sep, Monday–Friday 10–4.30, Sat/Sun 2–5, 1 Oct to 31 Mar, Mon–Fri 10–4.30, Sun 2–5.

No dogs in garden please. Cars may be parked only by garden wall.

Admission: £1 (honesty box).

Free admission to members of The National Trust for Scotland.

☻ The National Trust for Scotland

Inverewe Garden

Highland. On A832, by Poolewe,
6 miles north-east of Gairloch

Lochalsh Woodland Garden

Balmacara, Highland. A87, 3 miles east of
Kyle of Lochalsh. Bus: Skyeways from
Inverness & Glasgow; tel (01463) 710119

A MAGNIFICENT 50-acre Highland garden near Poolewe, in an impressive setting of mountains, moorland and sea-loch. When it was founded in 1862 by Osgood Mackenzie, only a dwarf willow grew where plants from many lands now flourish in a profusion as impressive as it is unexpected. Planned as a wild garden, it includes Australian tree ferns, exotic plants from China and a magnificent *Magnolia campbellii*. Good access for disabled visitors; wheelchairs available.

For further information tel (01455) 781200.

Open: garden, 15 Mar to 31 Oct, daily 9.30–9, 1 Nov to 14 Mar daily 9.30–5. Visitor Centre and shop, 15 Mar to 31 Oct, daily 9.30–5.30. Licensed restaurant, same dates, daily 10–5. Guided garden walks, 1 April to 30 Sep, Mon– Fri at 1.30. No dogs in garden. No shaded car parking.

Admission: adult £4.80, child/concession £3.20, adult/cruise party £3.80, child/school party £1, family £12.80.

Free admission to members of The National Trust for Scotland.

THIS 13-ACRE POLICY woodland enjoys a tranquil setting by the shore of Loch Alsh. The garden has developed a unique character, with collections of hardy ferns, fuchsias, hydrangeas, bamboos and rhododendrons. It is still developing, and new additions include plants from New Zealand and Tasmania.

For further information tel (01599) 566325.

Open: all year, daily 9–sunset. Kiosk (unstaffed), 1 Apr to 30 Sep, daily 9–5. Admission: adult £1, child/concession 50p (honesty box).

Free admission to members of The National Trust for Scotland.

☻ The National Trust for Scotland

Kellie Castle Garden

Fife. On B9171, 3 miles north of Pittenweem. Bus: limited service, tel Fife Scottish (01333) 426038

House of Dun Garden

Angus. On A935, 3 miles west of Montrose. Bus: Strathtay Buses, tel (01674) 672855

A DELIGHTFUL MODEL of a late Victorian garden, with box-edged paths, rose arches and many herbaceous plants and roses of the period, representing a style not found in any other Trust garden. Important work is being carried out at Kellie, with old varieties of vegetables and fruits being grown to ensure that a seed archive exists. The organic gardening methods used here make Kellie an inspiring garden to visit. Good access for disabled visitors: wheelchairs available.

For further information tel (01333) 720271.

Open: Castle, Good Friday to Easter Monday and 1 May to 30 Sep, daily 1.30–5.30; weekends in Oct 1.30–5.30 (last admission 4.45). Garden and grounds, all year, daily 9.30–sunset.

Admission: Castle and garden, adult £3.70, child/concession £2.50, adult party £3, child/ school party £1, family £9.90. Garden and grounds only, £1 (honesty box).
Free admission to members of The National Trust for Scotland.

W ILLIAM ADAM not only designed this beautiful country house, but also the landscape surrounding it. The restored walled garden displays lovely period herbaceous and rose borders while the avenues and the ha-ha are the original surviving features. *Wellingtonias* present a striking entrance to the north of the house and the Den offers a pleasant and restful woodland walk.

For further information tel (01674) 810264.

Open: house and shop, Good Friday to Easter Monday and 1 May to 30 Sep daily 1.30–5.30; weekends in Oct, 1.30–5.30 (last admission 5). Restaurant, same dates, but opens at 11. Garden and grounds, all year, daily 9.30–sunset.

Admission: house and garden, adult £3.70, child/concession £2.50, adult party £3, child/ school party £1, family £9.90. Garden and grounds only, £1 (honesty box).
Free admission to members of The National Trust for Scotland.

❦ The National Trust for Scotland

Leith Hall Garden

On B9002, 1 mile west of Kennethmont and 34 miles north-west of Aberdeen. Bus: infrequent service; tel Bluebird Buses (01224) 212266.

THIS ATTRACTIVE old country house, the earliest part of which dates from 1650, was the home of the Leith and Leith-Hay families for more than three centuries. The west garden was made by Mr and The Hon. Mrs Charles Leith-Hay around the beginning of the twentieth century; they also initiated many other improvements to the policies, which were later continued by a niece and her husband, Col and Mrs Derrick Gascoigne. The property was given to the Trust in 1945. The rock garden has been enhanced by the Scottish Rock Garden Club in celebration of their 150th anniversary. Toilet for disabled visitors.

For further information tel (01464) 831216.

Open: house and tearoom, Good Friday to Easter Monday and 1 May to 30 Sep, daily 1.30–5.30; weekends in Oct, 1.30 – 5.30 (last admission 4.45). Garden and grounds, all year, daily 9.30 – sunset.

Admission: adult £4.20, child/concession £2.80, adult party £3.40, child/school party £1, family £11.20. Garden and grounds only, adult £2, child/concession £1.30, adult party £1.60, child/ school party £1.
Free admission to members of The National Trust for Scotland.

Priorwood Garden and Dried Flower Shop

Borders. A6091, in Melrose. Bus: Lowland SMT from Edinburgh and Peebles; tel (0131) 663 9233

OVERLOOKED BY MELROSE Abbey's fifteenth-century ruins is this unique garden, where most of the plants are suitable for drying. With the help of volunteers, Priorwood markets a wide range of dried flower arrangements through its own dried flower shop. Visitors can also enjoy a stroll through the adjacent orchard which includes many varieties of historic fruit trees.

For further information tel (01896) 822493.

Open: 1 Apr to 30 Sep, Mon–Sat 10–5.30, Sun 1.30–5.30. 1 Oct to 24 Dec, Mon–Sat 10–4, Sun 1.30–4.

NTS Shop, 9 Jan to 31 Mar, Mon–Sat 12–4; 1 Apr to 24 Dec, Mon–Sat 10–5.30.Sun 1.30–5.30. Closed 31 Oct to 7 Nov for stocktaking.

Admission: £1 (honesty box).
Free admission to members of The National Trust for Scotland.

❦ The National Trust for Scotland

Pitmedden Garden

On A920, 1 mile west of Pitmedden village and 14 miles north of Aberdeen. Bus: infrequent service, tel Bluebird Buses (01224) 212266

Malleny Garden

Off A70, 6 miles west of Edinburgh city centre. Bus: LRT, tel (0131) 555 6363

THE CENTREPIECE OF this property is the Great Garden which was originally laid out in 1675 by Sir Alexander Seton, 1st Baronet of Pitmedden. The elaborate designs, now carefully re-created, were inspired by the garden at the Palace of Holyroodhouse, in Edinburgh. Fountains and sundials make excellent centrepieces to the garden, spectacularly filled in summer with 40,000 annual flowers. In the 100-acre estate is the renowned Museum of Farming Life. Wheelchair available.

For further information tel (01651) 842352.

Open: Garden, Visitor Centre, museum, tearoom, grounds & other facilities, 1 May to 30 Sep, daily 10–5.30, last admission 5.

Admission: adult £3.70, child/concession £2.50, adult party £3, child/school party £1, family £9.90.

Free admission to members of The National Trust for Scotland.

IN THE VILLAGE OF BALERNO, this three-acre walled garden beside seventeenth-century Malleny House (not open to visitors) provides a peaceful haven from the bustle of the nearby capital. Dominated by four 400 year-old clipped yew trees, this garden also features fine herbaceous borders and a large collection of old-fashioned roses. Malleny also houses the National Bonsai Collection for Scotland. Good access for disabled visitors.

For further information tel (0131) 449 2238 (office hours only).

Open: garden, 1 Apr to 31 Oct, daily 9.30–7; 1 Nov to 31 Mar, daily 9.30–4. House not open. Admission: £1 (honesty box).

Free admission to members of The National Trust for Scotland.

♛ The National Trust for Scotland
Threave Garden and Estate

Dumfries and Galloway. Off A75, 1 mile west of Castle Douglas.
Bus: McEwan's from Dumfries to Castle Douglas, tel (0345) 090510

THREAVE IS A GARDEN for all seasons. Best known for its spectacular springtime display of daffodils, there are also colourful summer displays from the herbaceous beds and borders, and striking autumn colour from the trees and the heather garden. Threave is also home to the Trust's School of Practical Gardening. Wheelchairs and electric battery car available.

For further information tel (01556) 502575.

Open: estate & garden, all year, daily 9.30–sunset. Walled garden and glasshouses, all year, daily 9.30–5. Visitor Centre, exhibition and shop, 1 Apr to 31 Oct, daily 9.30–5.30. Restaurant 10–5.

Admission: adult £4, child/concession £2.70, adult party £3.20, child/school party £1, family £10.70.

Free admission to members of The National Trust for Scotland.

HEAD GARDENERS' MEETING

The National Trust for Scotland arranges an annual meeting of Head Gardeners from Trust and privately owned gardens. The objects are to enable gardeners to maintain contact with others in their profession and to keep up-to-date with recent technical developments, and to allow visits to be made to local gardens or nurseries of interest. Meetings are normally based in a hall of residence.

Owners or staff from gardens which are open under Scotland's Gardens Scheme are welcome to apply for one of the limited places available. Please ask for further details from the Gardens Department, The National Trust for Scotland, 5 Charlotte Square, Edinburgh EH2 4DU, telephone (0131) 226 5922, fax (0131) 243 9444.

☰ The National Trust for Scotland
OTHER TRUST GARDEN PROPERTIES
(Free entry to members of The National Trust for Scotland)

BRODIE CASTLE, MORAY
A garden being restored to include a selection of the Brodie collection of daffodils and other varieties. Interesting mature trees and avenue. Open: castle, 1 Apr (or Good Friday if earlier) to 30 Sep, Mon-Sat 11-5.30, Sun 1.30-5.30; weekends in Oct, Sat 11-5.30, Sun 1.30-5.30 (last admission 4.30). Other times by appointment. Grounds, all year, daily 9.30 – sunset. Admission: adult £4.20, child/concession £2.80; adult party £3.40, child/ school party £1, family £11.20. Grounds only (outwith summer season's published opening times): £1 (honesty box).

BROUGHTON HOUSE, KIRKCUDBRIGHT, DUMFRIES AND GALLOWAY
A charming one-acre garden created by the artist E.A. Hornel between 1901 and 1933, which includes a 'Japanese-style' garden influenced by his many visits to the Far East. The garden includes many fine shrubs and herbaceous perennials. Open: house and garden, 1 Apr (or Good Friday if earlier) to 31 Oct, daily 1-5.30 (last admission 4.45)
Admission: adult £2.40, child/concession £1.60; adult party £1.90, child/school party £1, family £6.40.

CASTLE FRASER, ABERDEENSHIRE
A landscaped park with good trees and a walled garden which has been redesigned in a formal manner. Open: castle, Good Friday to Easter Monday, 1 May to 30 Jun and 1 to 30 Sep, daily 1.30-5.30; 1 July to 31 Aug, daily 11-5.30; weekends in Oct, 1.30-5.30 (last admission 4.45). Tearoom, dates as castle, but opens 12.30 when castle opens 1.30. Garden, all year, daily 9.30-6; grounds, all year, daily 9.30-sunset.
Admission: castle, garden and grounds, adult £4.20, child/concession £2.80; adult party £3.40, child/school party £1, family £11.20. Garden and grounds only, adult £2, child/concession £1.30; adult party £1.60, child/school party £1.

GREENBANK GARDEN, CLARKSTON, GLASGOW
A Gardening Advice Centre offering a series of regular guided walks. Extensive plant collection set in thematic displays and demonstration gardens including special garden for the disabled. Open: all year, daily 9.30-sunset, except 25/26 Dec and 1/2 Jan. Shop and tearoom, 1 Apr (or Good Friday if earlier) to 31 Oct, daily 11–5. 1 Nov to 31 Mar, Sat & Sun 2–4. House open 1 Apr to 31 Oct, Sundays only 2–4, and during special events (subject to functions in progress). No dogs in garden please.
Admission: adult £3, child/concession £2; adult party £2.40, child/school party £1, family £8.

THE HILL HOUSE, HELENSBURGH
The garden at The Hill House complements the finest example of the domestic architecture of Charles Rennie Mackintosh and is being restored to represent the designs of Walter Blackie with features by Mackintosh.Open: 1 Apr (or Good Friday if earlier) to 31 Oct, daily 1.30-5.30 (last admission 5); tearoom, 1.30-4.30. **Increasing visitor numbers are placing great strain on the structure of The Hill House, which was designed for domestic purposes. Access may be restricted at peak times and at the discretion of the Property Manager. Groups MUST pre-book.** Admission: house & garden, adult £5.80, child/conc. £3.90, family £15.50.

✿ The National Trust for Scotland
27 Beautiful Gardens to Visit

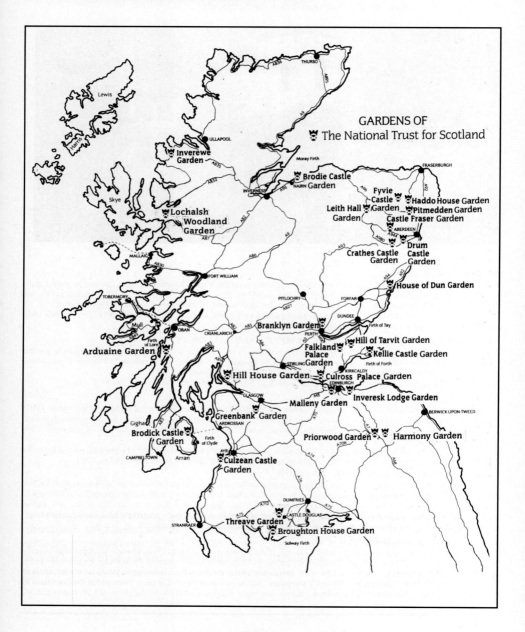

GARDENS OF
✿ The National Trust for Scotland

Inverewe Garden

Brodie Castle Garden

Lochalsh Woodland Garden

Fyvie Castle Garden
Haddo House Garden
Leith Hall Garden
Pitmedden Garden
Castle Fraser Garden

Drum Castle Garden

Crathes Castle Garden

House of Dun Garden

Branklyn Garden

Hill of Tarvit Garden

Arduaine Garden

Falkland Palace Garden

Kellie Castle Garden

Hill House Garden

Culross Palace Garden

Inveresk Lodge Garden

Malleny Garden

Greenbank Garden

Brodick Castle Garden

Priorwood Garden
Harmony Garden

Culzean Castle Garden

Threave Garden

Broughton House Garden

❦ The National Trust for Scotland
Scotland's leading conservation charity

THE NATIONAL TRUST FOR SCOTLAND belongs to you—to the people who love Scotland—and opens its properties for the enjoyment of all. That's why the brooding magnificence of Glencoe, the soaring mountains of Kintail, the peaceful beaches of Iona and so many great gardens are there for all to see and enjoy, protected for posterity.

At Inverewe Garden, palm trees grow on the same latitude as Labrador. From Brodick Castle Garden the rhododendrons win prizes at flower shows on both sides of the Atlantic. And at The NTS School of Practical Gardening, Threave, we train the head gardeners of the future.

But maintaining properties costs money. At Culzean Castle, Robert Adam's masterpiece overlooking the Clyde, the stonework is eroded by time and needs continual restoration. Repairs to the viaduct, and many other buildings on the estate now in progress, will take a team of stonemasons several years to complete. And the contents of our properties require as much attention and painstaking care as the exteriors. The Trust has its own bookbinding, metalwork, picture-framing and furniture restoration workshops.

Gardens need replanting, curtains frayed with age require to be repaired, and paths on mountains worn by feet need re-seeding. We repair leaky roofs, antiquated plumbing and rusting suits of armour. The list is endless. Each year it costs the Trust almost £14m to carry out this work, quite apart from any new projects we may wish to undertake. That's why we need your help.

If you love the countryside and have a special place in your heart for Scotland, you can help its preservation by joining The National Trust for Scotland. On the next page you will find another six good reasons for joining.

Welcome to 🛡 The National Trust for Scotland

The Trust was founded in 1931 by a small group of Scots, and today around 185,000 acres of countryside and gardens are in our care. The future of this very special heritage depends on the support of our members, and we look forward to welcoming you as a new member very soon!

Benefits of Membership

1 Free admission to our beautiful gardens and properties throughout Scotland, plus over 300 properties of The National Trust in England, Wales and Northern Ireland, and overseas.

2 Our quarterly colour magazine, *Heritage Scotland*, with lists of events, winter activities and a host of opportunities for you to enjoy.

3 For those who would like to do a little more, details of gardens and countryside guided walks, and of how to join one of our Members' support groups.

4 Priority booking for our holiday cottages, and an opportunity to book for our conservation and adventure base camps for groups, St Kilda work parties, and Thistle Camps for young people. Details of our Cruises.

5 Our annual full colour illustrated handbook listing opening times and facilities.

6 Facilities at our properties for all the family— grandparents, parents and children—including shops with our specially designed range of goods— and tearooms when you need to take the weight off your feet.

The National Trust for Scotland is a charity, independent of Government, supported by 230,000 members

JOIN us now – it's easy and terrific value for money

Membership Enrolment Form   Rates valid until 31 October 1998

☐ Member: £25.00 or more per annum.

☐ Family: £42.00 or more per annum. Two adults at one address (and any of their children or grandchildren, under 18).

☐ Life: £500.00 or more (includes cardholder's children under 18 and a guest).

☐ 25 & under: £10.00 or more per annum. Please give date of birth __/__/__

Over 60s may join at a discount.

UK residents: Senior Member £17.00 ☐   Joint Senior £28.00 ☐   Senior Life £335.00 ☐
Education, non-profit making societies and Corporate Commercial rates available on request.

I enclose remittance for/please charge my Credit Card £_____ Expiry date __/__

Visa/Access/American
Express/JCB/Mastercard/Switch No:

Please print

Mr/Mrs/Miss/Ms Surname_____Initials_____

Address:_____

_____

_____Postcode:_____

FOR NTS USE ONLY		
MEMBERSHIP NO.		
TYPE	SOURCE	
	214	
DAY	MONTH	YEAR
Amount received		
£		

Please send to: Membership Services, The National Trust for Scotland, 5 Charlotte Square, Edinburgh EH2 4DU
Tel (0131) 243 9555 Fax (0131) 243 9589

THE FINER SIDE OF SCOTTISH LIFE

An affordable, comfortable, year round extra room designed and crafted in Scotland, using timber or UPVC. A Cairn Conservatory will extend and complement your home for years to come.

- Built in Scotland to suit the Scottish climate

- Widely varied 'Standard' designs and a 'Made to Measure' range, individually designed to suit awkward situations

- We offer Full build service – all trades from Planning to completion

- Free Survey, Design Drawings and Quotation

- 'Maintenance Free' roofs in toughened glass or polycarbonate

- High security multi-point locking systems

- 10 year Insurance Backed Guarantee available

- Wide selection of Cane furniture and blinds

Cairn Conservatories and a range of Cane Furniture are available for personal inspection at our Showroom at:

Cairn Conservatories Ltd.
Killearn Mill, Killearn, by Glasgow G63 9LQ

or Telephone for Full Colour Brochure.
Tel: 01360 550922   Fax: 01360 550616
Showroom open 7 days a week
Opening Hours – Weekdays: 9.00am – 5.00pm.
Week-ends: 1.00pm – 4.00pm

CONSERVATORIES

ROYAL BOTANIC GARDEN EDINBURGH

The Royal Botanic Garden Edinburgh displays its living collections in four glorious gardens – Edinburgh, Younger, Logan and Dawyck.

ROYAL BOTANIC GARDEN EDINBURGH

Scotland's Premier Garden

Discover the wonders of the plant kingdom in Scotland's National Botanic Garden. Plants from around the world are displayed in over 28 hectares of beautifully landscaped grounds.

- •Rock Garden •Pringle Chinese Collection
- •Woodland Gardens •Arboretum
- •Glasshouse Experience – featuring Britain's Tallest Palm House
- •Botanics Shop •Terrace Cafe •Dill's Snack Bar
- •Guided Tours

Royal Botanic Garden Edinburgh, 20A Inverleith Row, Edinburgh EH3 5LR.
One mile north of the city centre, off the A902.
Tel: 0131 552 7171. Fax: 0131 552 0382.

Open daily (except 25 December & 1 January) from 9.30am. Closing times:– February, 5pm; March, 6pm; April–August, 7pm; September, 6pm; October, 5pm; November–January, 4pm.

ADMISSION FREE • DONATIONS WELCOME

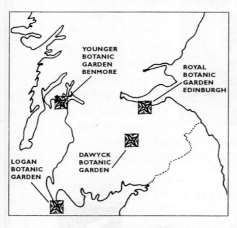

FRIENDS OF THE
ROYAL BOTANIC GARDEN EDINBURGH

Joining the Friends enables you to support the vital work of Scotland's National Botanic Garden.

Through the Friends you can enjoy a close relationship with this great institution and learn about the fascinating world of gardening, plants and science. You can participate in Friends events where you meet like-minded people: there are lectures, guided walks, garden visits, plant auctions of special Garden plants and plant sales. Membership entitles you to free entry to Younger, Logan, Dawyck, RBG Kew and Wakehurst Place.

Your membership can make a positive difference – it costs £20 for individuals, £25 for families and just £5 for students.

JOIN THE FRIENDS AND SUPPORT THE GARDEN

Come to the Friends Plant Sale on Sunday 7 June, 2.30pm, at the Garden Nursery, Inverleith Avenue South. All welcome.

Write to The Friends Office, Royal Botanic Garden Edinburgh, 20A Inverleith Row, Edinburgh EH3 5LR.
Tel: 0131 552 5339.

YOUNGER BOTANIC GARDEN BENMORE

A Botanical Paradise

Marvel at nature's giants.
•Avenue of Giant Redwoods •Over 250 rhododendron species
•World famous collections of trees and shrubs
•James Duncan Cafe •Botanics Shop
•Shop and Cafe are open to non-Garden visitors and the Cafe is
available for hire.

SPECIAL SCOTLAND'S GARDENS SCHEME OPENING 26 APRIL 1998.

**Younger Botanic Garden Benmore, Dunoon, Argyll PA23 8QU.
7 miles north of Dunoon, on the A815. Tel: 01369 706261. Fax: 01369 706369.**

LOGAN BOTANIC GARDEN

Scotland's Most Exotic Garden

Come and see tender exotics which can be found
in few other gardens in Britain.
•Tree ferns •Cabbage palms •Unusual shrubs & climbers
•Tender perennials •Discovery Centre •Self-guided tours
•Botanics Shop •Salad Bar

SPECIAL SCOTLAND'S GARDENS SCHEME OPENING 24 MAY 1998.

**Logan Botanic Garden, Port Logan, Wigtownshire DG9 9ND.
14 miles south of Stranraer, off the B7075. Tel: 01776 860231. Fax: 01776 860333.**

DAWYCK BOTANIC GARDEN

Spectacular Woodland Garden

Discover Dawyck's secrets as you explore its wonderful woodlands.
•Mature specimen trees – some over 40 metres tall •"Non-
flowering" plants in the Cryptogamic Sanctuary and Reserve
•Landscaped burnside walks
•Conservatory with light refreshments and thoughtfully selected gifts,
books, souvenirs, local crafts and plants

SPECIAL SCOTLAND'S GARDENS SCHEME OPENING 10 MAY 1998.

**Dawyck Botanic Garden, Stobo, Peeblesshire EH45 9JU.
8 miles southwest of Peebles, on the B712. Tel: 01721 760254. Fax: 01721 760214.**

**Specialist Gardens open: 1 March to 31 October, 9.30am–6pm (and at other times by arrangement).
Admission: Adult £3.00, Concession £2.50, Child £1.00, Family £7.00.
Season tickets with special benefits are available.**

CLAN DONALD

VISITOR CENTRE

The 'Garden of Skye' nestles in a sheltered corner of Skye's Sleat peninsula. The 40 acres of woodland garden are based around a 19th century collection of exotic trees. Much of the garden has been restored, displaying plants from around the world. New features include the ponds, rockery, herbaceous borders and terrace walk

'MUSEUM OF THE ISLES'   COUNTRYSIDE RANGER SERVICE   GIFT SHOPS   RESTAURANT   LUXURY SELF CATERING COTTAGES

CLAN DONALD VISITOR CENTRE
Telephone: 01471 844305 Fax: 01471 844275

Visit GLEN GRANT
DISTILLERY & GARDEN

Discover the mysteries of a very
special malt whisky, and enjoy a stroll up the
enchanting garden, carefully restored to
its original Victorian glory.

Opening Times

Mid March to end October
Monday - Saturday 10.00am - 4.00pm   Sunday 11.30am - 4.00pm
June to end September
Remains open until 5.00pm daily

Admission - £2.50 includes £2.00 voucher redeemable in distillery shop
against the purchase of a 70cl. bottle of whisky.
Under 18s free. Children under the age of 8 are not admitted to
production areas but are welcome in the centre and garden.

Glen Grant Distillery & Garden, Rothes, Aberlour AB38 7BS
Telephone: 01542 78 3318   Fax: 01542 78 3304

The Garden
4 July 1998

Entries are now invited for our annual auction of garden furniture, statuary, paintings, books, antique tools and ephemera.

'The Botanical Magazine of Flower Garden Displayed' by William Curtis
Plate illustrated "Amaryllis Aurea"
Sold in The Garden sale July 1997 for £897

*Enquiries: Campbell Armour on 0141 221 8377
or Neil Froggatt on 0131 225 2266*

Quality Garden Tours

Brightwater Holidays are Scotland's specialist Garden Tour Operators.
Our fully inclusive itineraries combine the famous and grand gardens with
small and private gardens - most tours also visit specialist nurseries.
Travel by comfortable coach from a variety of local pick-up points throughout
Scotland and the UK. Tours for 1998 include:

The Literary Gardens of England
Highland & Island Gardens - the Gardens of Argyll
In an Irish Garden
Gardens of the Far North including the Castle of Mey
Norfolk and the Lavender Harvest
The Chelsea Flower Show
Monet's Garden and the Gardens of Normandy
Italy's Gardens of Ninfa
Dutch Bulbfields Cruise & Tresco & Cornish Gardens

If you have your own group and are looking for a tailor made itinerary we are
happy to work to suit your interests and budget. For brochure and full details
contact:

BRIGHTWATER HOLIDAYS LIMITED
Eden Park House, Cupar, Fife KY15 4HS
Tel: 01334 657155 Fax: 01334 657144
Email: BrightwaterHolidays@compuserve.com

DRUMMOND CASTLE GARDENS, PERTHSHIRE

Scotland's most important formal gardens, among the finest in Europe. The upper terraces offer stunning views and overlook a magnificent parterre celebrating the saltire, family heraldry and the famous multiplex sundial by John Milne, Master Mason to Charles I.

OPEN EASTER WEEKEND, THEN DAILY MAY 1ST TO OCTOBER 31ST 2PM - 6PM (LAST ENTRY 5PM)

Tel: 01764 681257   Fax: 01764 681550
Entrance 2 miles south of Crieff on A822
Featured recently in United Artists' "Rob Roy"

Finlaystone

Overlooking the Clyde 10 min west of Glasgow Airport on A8 west of Langbank

Eye-Opener Centre with ▼ Shop ▼ Clan MacMillan Centre ▼ Celtic Art Exhibition ▼"Dolly Mixture" Doll Collection

Gardens with richly varied   **Woodland walks** with play   **Mansion House** with historic connection
and unusual plants and pond   and picnic areas and waterfalls   with Robert Burns and John Knox

OPEN THROUGHOUT THE YEAR 10.30 – 5.00
Historic House with Victorian Kitchen open Sundays April – August
Tours at 2.30pm and 3.30pm or by appointment
Lunch and tea in the **"Celtic Tree"** in the Walled Garden (Open April – September)
Group bookings welcome Tel: 01475 540285 (House) or 01475 540505 (Ranger)
Finlaystone, Langbank, Renfrewshire PA14 6TJ

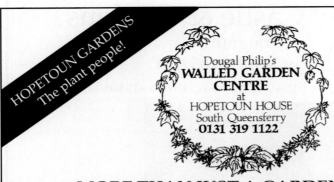

146

THE BUCCLEUCH ESTATES

invite you to visit

BOWHILL HOUSE & COUNTRY PARK, Nr Selkirk (Scottish Borders)

18/19th century house in beautiful countryside. Outstanding art collection, fine French furniture and relics of Duke of Monmouth, Sir Walter Scott and Queen Victoria.

Exciting Adventure Woodland Play Area. Audio-visual Visitor Centre. Nature Trails. Picnic Areas. Restored Victorian Kitchen. Tea Room. Gift Shop.

OPEN 1998

House	1–31 July daily 1–4.30
Country Park	25 April to 31 August incl. daily except Fridays 12-5. Open on Fridays during July with House.
Telephone No.	Selkirk (01750) 22204

Off A708 – St. Mary's Loch-Moffat Road 3 miles west of Selkirk. Edinburgh 42 miles, Glasgow 75 miles, Berwick 43 miles, Newcastle 80 miles, Carlisle 56 miles.

Bowhill House

DRUMLANRIG CASTLE GARDENS & COUNTRY PARK Nr Thornhill, Dumfriesshire (South-west Scotland)

Castle built 1679-91 on a 15th century Douglas stronghold. Set in parkland ringed by wild hills. French furniture. Paintings by Rembrandt, Holbein and Leonardo. Bonnie Prince Charlie relics. Gift shop. Tea Room. Exciting Adventure Woodland Play Area. Picnic Sites. Nature Trails. Birds of Prey Centre. Visitors Centre. Craft Centre.

OPEN 1998

Castle and Country Park	Saturday 2 May to Monday 31 August. 10,11,12 July & 24–31 August by appointment only. Castle daily 12–4.Gardens daily 11–5 throughout.
Telephone:	(01848) 330248 - Castle (01848) 331555 - Country Park

Off A76, 4 miles north of Thornhill. Glasgow 56 miles, Dumfries 18 miles, Edinburgh 56 miles, Carlisle 51 miles.

Drumlanrig Castle

BOUGHTON HOUSE, Nr Kettering (Northamptonshire)

Northamptonshire home of the Dukes of Buccleuch and their Montagu ancestors since 1528. Important art collection, French and English Furniture and Tapestries. "A vision of Louis XIV's Versailles transported to England".

Exciting Adventure Woodland Play Area. Nature Trail. Tea Room. Gift Shop. Garden Centre.

Further details on www.boughton house.org.uk

OPEN 1998

Grounds	1May–15 September incl. 1–5 daily, except Fridays.
House and Grounds	1 August–1 September, 2–5 daily. (Grounds open 1 pm)
Telephone No.	Kettering (01536) 515731.

Off A43, 3 miles north of Kettering. Northampton 17 miles, Cambridge 45 miles, Coventry 44 miles, Peterborough 32 miles, Leicester 26 miles, London 50 minutes by train.

Boughton House

DALKEITH PARK, Nr Edinburgh (Lothian Region)

Dalkeith Palace not open to public

Nature Trails. Woodland and riverside walks in the extensive grounds of Dalkeith Palace. Tunnel Walk. Adam Bridge. Fascinating Architecture. Exciting Adventure Woodland Play Area. Picnic Area. Barbecue facilities. Information Centre. Scottish farm animals. Ranger service. Come to our new Cafeteria/Shop in our restored Adam stable.

OPEN 1998

Grounds	26 March–29 October incl. 10 am-6 pm daily & weekends in winter.
Telephone Nos.	0131-663 5684, 665 3277 or 654 1666

Access from east end of Dalkeith High Street.

Off A68, 3 miles from Edinburgh City Boundary.

Dalkeith Palace from the Nature Trail

Parties welcome at all these estates (Special terms and extended opening times for pre-booked parties over 20).
All the houses have special facilities for wheelchair visitors.

Get the most out of your garden with the help of the Royal Horticultural Society

save £5 if you join today

Whatever your gardening experience, there are times when having some expert advice would be very useful. Membership of the RHS is like having a panel of experts on hand whenever you need it. From practical advice in *The Garden* magazine to instructional model gardens and inspirational flower shows – there's something for every gardener.

Ten good reasons to join today

- Save £5 by joining now
- Free monthly magazine *The Garden* delivered to your door
- Reduced price tickets to Scotland's National Gardening Show (saving up to £12)
- Free unlimited access for you and a guest, to RHS Gardens Wisley, Rosemoor and Hyde Hall
- Free unlimited access for you to a further 23 beautiful gardens across the UK
- Reduced price tickets and members' only days to the Chelsea Flower Show and the RHS Great Summer Flower Show at Hampton Court Palace
- Reduced price tickets to BBC Gardeners' World Live, Malvern Spring and Autumn Shows
- Free gardening advice from Britain's experts
- Free seeds from RHS Garden Wisley
- Privileged access to over 250 talks and demonstrations across the UK

The RHS is not only the world's premier gardening organisation; it is your key to a world of gardening delights throughout the year. Simply complete the form below or return your details to us today to save £5

Gardens of Scotland – RHS membership offer

☐ **I would like to enjoy membership at the special reduced rate of £28 saving £5 (normal price of membership £33).**

☐ **I enclose a cheque made payable to The Royal Horticultural Society for £28.**

PLEASE COMPLETE IN BLOCK CAPITALS

YOUR DETAILS

Title ....Initials ....Surname...

Address ....

....

Postcode...Daytime Tel. No. ....

Code 1011

Please return your completed form and cheque to : RHS Membership Department, 80 Vincent Square, London.SW1P 2PE. Offer expires 31 October 1998. Please allow 28 days for delivery of your membership pack.

The secret garden centre

Nestling in a sheltered Strathmore location beneath Dunnichen Hill by the Vinny Burn is a unique garden centre with everything you need to create an inspired garden. Discover something new from our exciting and unusual plant varieties, or choose an old cottage garden favourite. We're bamboo and ornamental grass enthusiasts too!

Top quality plants are our business.

During your visit, pop into the Topiary Coffee Shop for a tempting snack or mouth-watering cake.

We're not easy to find, but well worth a visit. Only 4 miles from House of Pitmuies.

Bowriefauld Garden Centre & Nurseries Limited,

Bowriefauld, By Letham, Forfar, Angus, DD8 2LX.

01307 818356

155

INDEX TO GARDENS

♿ Denotes gardens suitable for wheelchairs

\# Denotes gardens opening for the first time
or re-opening after several years.

INDEX TO ADVERTISERS

GARDENS OF SCOTLAND
1999

Order your copy now and it will be posted to you on publication in February.

✂ --

To: SCOTLAND'S GARDENS SCHEME
31 CASTLE TERRACE, EDINBURGH EH1 2EL

Please send _____ copy / copies of "Gardens of Scotland 1999" at £3.75 each, inclusive of postage, *as soon as it is available.* I enclose a cheque / postal order payable to Scotland's Gardens Scheme.

Name ....

Address ....

....

.... Post Code ....

NOTES